Pack of Lies

A Play

D1575134

Hugh Whitemore

Samuel French - London
New York - Toronto - Hollywood

For Judy

CHARACTERS

Bob
Barbara
Julie
Helen
Peter
Stewart
Thelma
Sally

The play takes place in a suburb of London during the autumn and winter of 1960–61

The main events of the story are true

PACK OF LIES

First presented by Michael Redington in association with Bernard Sandler and Eddie Kulukundis at the Theatre Royal, Brighton, on 11th October, 1983, and subsequently at the Lyric Theatre, London, on 26th October, 1983, with the following cast:

Bob Jackson	Michael Williams
Barbara Jackson	Judi Dench
Julie Jackson	Eva Griffith
Helen Kroger	Barbara Leigh-Hunt
Peter Kroger	Larry Hoodekoff
Stewart	Richard Vernon
Thelma	Elizabeth Bell
Sally	Penny Ryder

Directed by Clifford Williams
Designed by Ralph Koltai

FOREWORD

In 1961 Helen and Peter Kroger were found guilty of spying for the Russians and were sentenced to twenty years' imprisonment. In 1969 they were exchanged for a Briton jailed in Moscow, and flew off to Poland amidst a great hullabaloo in the press.

Shortly after the Krogers' release, Gay Search, a young journalist, was having dinner with Cedric Messina, who was then producing BBC's *Play of the Month* series. Conversation touched on the Krogers, and Miss Search said, "I know them. In fact, they were our neighbours." She then told Messina the full story of her involvement with the Krogers and how her family had played a key part in their capture. Messina was amazed and excited by the story. The following day he telephoned me to say that he believed he had unearthed a good subject for a television play. Miss Search and I met, discussed the project with Messina, and I was subsequently commissioned to write a play, which was entitled *Act of Betrayal*. It was transmitted in January 1971 and was well received by both the press and the public.

Long after the play's production, the subject and its implications stayed in my mind. The television script had adhered very closely to known facts and, as is always the case with documentary drama, the scope for imaginative development of characters and situations was limited. In addition to the themes of loyalty and deception, I became increasingly preoccupied with the role of the ordinary citizen in our society. It is ever possible for the average, relatively powerless, man or woman to make anything more than a token stand against officialdom? It is not potentially risky to allow the state (albeit for well-argued reasons) greater moral licence than the individual? Or is it, perhaps, naïve to expect more than an approximate degree of truthfulness from governments and their spokesmen?

With these thoughts in mind, I decided to rework the basic story of *Act of Betrayal* in a longer, less restricted, more fictionalized form. *Pack of Lies* is the result.

Before starting work on the play, I wrote to the man who was in charge of M.I.5 day-by-day handling of the case (the character called Stewart is not, I hasten to add, a portrait of this man, but an entirely fictional creation). In my letter, I made it clear that all I wanted was an informal conversation and that I was not hoping for any startling or indiscreet disclosures. The gentleman replied most courteously, but regretted that he was unable to meet me. He said that his "former masters" had imposed "a total embargo on interviews of any sort". Although I detected traces of ironic humour in the tone of his letter, I couldn't help asking myself a few more questions: Who are these "former masters"? Who gave them their authority? How can we, the general public, be sure that they are acting wisely? And if not, how can we control them?

Gay Search and her father helped me most generously in the writing of this play; my thanks to them, and to Clifford Williams, Sarah Moorehead and Michael Redington, who, in addition to his many managerial duties, thought of the excellent title. My thanks also to Arthur Cantor.

Hugh Whitemore

ACT I

Bob enters and addresses the audience. He is in his forties. He wears a grey suit

Bob I was out in the garden when I heard the doorbell. It was a Saturday afternoon. I was just pottering about, sweeping up leaves and so on. Barbara and Julie had gone shopping. When I opened the front door I found a man and a woman smiling at me. They were holding a Bible and some religious pamphlets. "We've come to bring you the key to great happiness," the man said. "Thanks very much," I said, "but I'm happy enough as it is"—and shut the door quickly before they had a chance to say another word. They walked away slowly, still smiling—I could see them through the window. I suppose they were used to having doors slammed in their faces. Later, when I was back in the garden, I thought to myself, "Well, it's true—I am happy—it's true." And for a moment I stood there, grinning from ear to ear, just because I felt happy for no particular reason. (*He grins*) It was marvellous.

Barbara enters the kitchen

The Lights come up. Day

A small semi-detached house near London, typical of the thousands of suburban homes that were built between the wars. R *is the sitting-room: tiled fireplace, net curtains at the bay window, chintz-covered chairs and sofa, small tables, a sideboard, a radiogram, framed paintings of flowers on the walls.* L *is the kitchen, with a back door leading to the garden. Upstage is the entrance hall and front door, which has a stained-glass panel. A telephone stands on a table beside the stairs leading to the unseen bedrooms*

Bob goes to the kitchen where his wife, Barbara, is preparing breakfast. He sits at the table, picks up the newspaper, and pours himself some tea

Barbara What's Julie doing?
Bob I don't know. Getting dressed.
Barbara It's almost eight o'clock.
Bob Yes, I told her.
Barbara (*calling*) Julie! (*To Bob*) I do wish we didn't have this awful rush every morning.
Bob It doesn't matter, I'll give her a lift.
Barbara Why can't we have breakfast like civilized human beings for a change?

Bob Well, never mind.

Barbara (*irritated*) Never mind ...!

Julie enters—a teenager wearing school uniform

Julie Sorry.

Barbara About time.

Julie Sorry.

Barbara Every morning it's the same—why do you do it? Rush, rush, rush.

Julie I didn't hear the alarm.

Barbara That's because you went to bed so late.

Julie It wasn't that late.

Bob When I was your age I was in bed by half-past nine and no arguing.

Julie That's just silly.

Bob No, it's not, you need your rest.

Julie What's the point of going to bed if I can't sleep?

Barbara If you went to bed earlier you'd go to sleep earlier.

Julie No, I wouldn't.

Bob You might.

Julie No, I wouldn't. I don't feel sleepy at night—only in the mornings.

Barbara Oh, Julie.

Julie It's not my fault——

Bob No, nothing ever is.

Julie —it's biological.

Bob What is?

Barbara Shall I make toast?

Bob What's biological?

Julie Feeling tired. Has the postman been?

Barbara Julie ...

Julie What?

Barbara Do you want some toast?

Julie No, thanks.

Barbara You must have something before you go to school.

Julie I'll have an apple.

Barbara That's not enough.

Bob What's biological about feeling tired?

Julie It all depends when you reach your peak. You're either a day person
   or a night person. (*Biting into an apple*) You're day people and I'm not.

Bob Trust you to be different.

Julie It's true. These apples aren't very nice.

Barbara Have a glass of milk, then.

Julie Isn't there anything else?

Bob Tea?

Julie Not at breakfast time.

Bob What's wrong with tea?

Julie Couldn't we have coffee or fruit juice or something?

Barbara Fruit juice ...?

Julie People don't have tea with breakfast anymore. It's so old-
   fashioned——

Bob What are you talking about?

Julie —and boring.
Bob What is?
Barbara Have some cornflakes. You like cornflakes.

The front doorbell rings

Julie I'll go.

Julie goes to the front door

Bob What on earth is she talking about?
Barbara Try and get her to eat something.
Bob She won't listen to me.

Julie opens the front door

>*Helen and Peter enter; they are carrying a large object (in fact, an artist's easel) wrapped in a tablecloth. Helen is a tall, large-boned American in her forties; she invariably wears slacks and sweaters. Peter, her husband, is about fifty, also an American; he too prefers casual clothes*

Helen Hi, sweetheart.
Julie Hello, Auntie Helen—Uncle Peter.
Bob (*to Barbara*) God, it's Helen, that's all we need.
Barbara Ssshhh.
Helen (*to Peter*) Don't push, for Chrissake!
Peter Sorry.

Julie is staring at the tablecloth-shrouded object

Julie What's that?
Helen Surprise, surprise! (*To Peter*) Back off! You're pushing it right into my goddam ribs.
Peter Sorry, honey.
Helen (*to Julie*) My husband is physically maladjusted, do you know that?
Peter (*grinning*) Maladjusted . . .?
Helen I don't mean maladjusted. Will you open the door please, sweetheart? He malfunctions. What do you call it? No coordination——

Bob pushes back his chair and stands up

Bob What's going on out there?
Helen Tell him to lift something—he goes right ahead and pushes it.
Peter That's not true.
Helen Mind that table—Jesus! (*Entering the sitting-room*) Over there—put it over there. Hi, Bob, where is she?
Bob She's in the kitchen getting the breakfast.
Helen Barbara, where are you? Barbara!

>*Barbara enters from the kitchen*

Barbara I'm here.

With a flourish, Helen gestures towards the easel and sings "Happy Birthday". Barbara stares in amazement. Peter smiles

Peter We couldn't find any paper big enough—hence the tablecloth.

Julie and Bob are giggling

Helen Go on—open it up.
Barbara (*trying not to laugh*) Oh, Helen . . .
Helen What's the matter?
Barbara It's not my birthday.
Helen Whaat?!

Peter shouts with laughter

Barbara It's next week. The twenty-ninth.
Peter What did I say? What did I tell you?
Helen Don't give me that, you said no such thing.
Peter "When's Barbara's birthday?" you said, and I said the twenty-ninth.
Helen You didn't.
Peter I did.
Helen You didn't.
Peter I did.
Helen (*turning to Barbara*) The twenty-ninth . . .?
Barbara That's right.
Helen (*to Peter*) You said the nineteenth.
Peter I didn't.
Helen You did.
Peter I swear to you. I did not.
Helen What are you trying to do to me? Jesus! It's like that goddam film—
  what's it called?—you know—Ingrid Bergman thinks she's going crazy,
  but it's her husband all the time—it's Cary Grant or James Mason or
  someone——
Peter Charles Boyer.
Helen He keeps telling her the wrong things so she thinks she's going
  crazy—is that what you're trying to do? (*To Bob*) He said the nineteenth. I
  know he said the nineteenth.
Peter If I did, I'm sorry—my mistake, okay? (*To Barbara*) Come on, you'd
  better open it up.
Barbara Shall I?
Helen I'm sure as hell not taking it back home again.
Julie Yes, go on.
Barbara What is this, some terrible joke?
Peter Let me give you a hand, it's a bit tricky. (*He unwraps the easel*)
Julie Wow!
Helen Well—do you like it?

*Barbara stands speechless for a moment, unable to find the words to express
her delight*

Peter It's an easel. For your paintings.
Helen She knows it's an easel, you dumdum. (*To Barbara*) Come on—don't
  keep us in suspense—do you like it or don't you?
Barbara I love it. It's wonderful. I don't know what to say.

Peter Now that you're going to these art classes, we thought you ought to have all the regular ... (*He completes the sentence with a gesture towards the easel*)

Barbara You shouldn't have done this, it's much too extravagant.

Helen (*overlapping*) Now, don't give me any of that English phoney-baloney about "Oh, you shouldn't have," and all that horseshit. You're my very good and dear friend, Barbara, and if I want to buy you a fancy birthday present, no-one's going to stop me, okay? Okay?

Barbara (*smiling*) Okay.

Helen And if it ain't your birthday, who cares—what the hell—we'll call it a thanksgiving present.

Julie Thanksgiving for what?

Helen Thanksgiving for what ...? (*Improvising rapidly*) Okay, I'll tell you what. How many people are there living in London? Six million? Eight? Let's say six, okay? So that means it was something like three-million-to-one that we'd find ourselves living across the street from wonderful folk like you—and if that ain't the cause for some kind of thanksgiving, I don't know what is!

Barbara laughs and embraces Helen

Barbara Oh, Helen, dear Helen—you're priceless!

The Lights fade

Barbara, Helen, Bob, Julie and Peter exit

Stewart enters and addresses the audience. He is in his forties, wearing a raincoat and a dark blue suit. He might be mistaken for an averagely successful provincial solicitor

Stewart Eventually our investigations led us to a street in Ruislip. It was autumn, nineteen-sixty. Ruislip, I should explain, is a suburb of London. It lies to the northwest of the metropolis and is one of the places one drives through on the way to Oxford. That is how I remember it, at any rate: as somewhere glimpsed briefly through car windows, generally at dusk, generally in the rain—neat rows of semi-detached houses; small front gardens, each with its square of lawn and herbaceous border; bay windows; clipped hedges; and every so often, where the downstairs curtains have yet to be drawn, the blueish flickering light of a television set. And that, since all stories have to begin somewhere, is where this particular story began for me—or rather this particular chapter of this particular story, for the case as a whole had been occupying my attention for several months. It is, by the way, by and large—true.

The Lights fade

Stewart exits

The Lights come up. Dusk

Barbara and Helen are coming downstairs. Barbara is carrying a dress;

Helen is wearing an almost-completed dress (some of it is still only pinned together), and carrying the dress she arrived in

Helen Where do you want me to go?

Barbara In the sitting-room.

Helen (*going into the sitting-room*) Jesus, it's cold in here. You ought to get central heating.

Barbara (*switching on the electric fire*) Well, one day.

Helen drapes her own dress over a chair and positions herself in the centre of the room

Helen Okay, what do you want me to do?

Barbara Just stand still. I want to make sure that it fits all right.

Helen God, you're a fast worker.

Barbara I've got to get a move on if it's going to be ready for Christmas. Hold your arm up. Let me look at the sleeve.

Helen Like this? (*She extends her arm*)

Barbara Yes, that's fine.

Thus for a moment, Barbara and Helen stand face-to-face, with their arms extended, almost like ballroom dancers, Helen, realizing this similarity, suddenly grabs Barbara by the waist and whirls her across the room

Helen Hey, come on—let's dance!

Barbara (*protesting but laughing*) Stop it, Helen, stop it.

Helen (*singing*) "Shall we dance, pom pom pom pom—Shall we dance deedle-eedle"—come on.

Barbara (*laughing*) Oh, Helen, you are a fool.

Helen Do you ever go dancing? I never go dancing. I used to love dancing when I was a girl.

Barbara Where could you dance round here?

Helen We could organize something. Why not? We could have dances in the afternoon. What are they called? Tea dances. We could have tea dances in Cranley Drive.

Barbara Who'd come?

Helen Lots of people, I bet.

Barbara All the men are at work.

Helen Okay, so we could ask some of the boys from school.

Barbara They're a bit young.

Helen Who cares? They're a good-looking bunch.

Barbara Some of them.

Helen That guy Julie likes—he's really good-looking.

Barbara You mean Malcolm Granger?

Helen Don't you think he's good-looking?

Barbara He's completely irresponsible. Have you seen the way he races around on that motorbike of his? He'll get himself killed one of these days.

Helen If you're worried, tell her.

Barbara I can't.

Helen Why not?

Barbara She thinks I worry about everything.

Helen She's right, you do.

Barbara I try not to.

Helen It's your nature, you can't help it—she knows that, I know that, we all know that. (*She squeezes Barbara's hand comfortingly*) Now, listen, here's what to do if you're worried: you tell her she's too young to go riding about on motorcycles.

Barbara I've told her that already.

Helen Then she won't. She's a good girl. She'll do what you say.

Barbara, unconvinced, says nothing. Helen grins

You know something? Malcolm Granger has a beautiful body. I saw him at the pool last summer. Beautiful! Maybe I should lure him round to the house when Peter goes to one of his antiquarian book sales. What do you think? Shall I introduce him to the more sophisticated charms of an older woman?

Barbara does not respond; she is preoccupied with her anxieties about Julie

Barbara I wish you'd say something to her.

Helen Say what?

Barbara About going on the motorbike.

Helen looks at Barbara

Helen You really are worried.

Barbara Yes, I am.

Helen What can I say?

Barbara She'd listen to you.

Helen What about Bob? Why doesn't he talk to her?

Barbara You know what Bob's like. She can't do a thing wrong as far as he's concerned. (*Brief pause*) Please. There's no-one else I can ask ... Please.

Helen hesitates

Helen Okay.

Barbara (*relieved*) Would you?

Helen Okay, if it'll make you any happier.

Barbara Well, it would.

Helen Okay.

Barbara Thanks. I hate asking.

Helen Don't be silly. (*Deliberately changing the mood*) It's beautiful, this dress—really beautiful. You're such a clever girl, Barbara. You do so many things real good. You've got golden hands.

Barbara What a funny thing to say.

Helen Well, it's true.

Julie opens the front door; She's wearing a raincoat, scarf, and gloves over her school uniform; She carries a satchel

Julie (*calling*) Mum!

Barbara (*calling*) In here, Julie. (*Whispering to Helen*) Don't tell her I asked you to say anything.
Helen Of course I won't. Don't worry.

Julie enters the sitting-room and kisses Barbara

Julie Hello, Mum. Hello, Auntie Helen.
Helen Hi, Julie, sweetheart.
Barbara How was choir practice?
Julie Boring. Every year it's *The Messiah*. If only we could do something different. It's so boring doing the same old thing year after year.
Barbara Everything's boring as far as you're concerned.
Julie The dress looks smashing.
Helen Doesn't it? (*She starts to change dresses*)
Barbara It's quite an easy pattern.
Helen Don't be so modest. Be proud. If I could make a dress like this, I'd be really proud of myself.
Barbara You could if you tried.
Helen Honey, I couldn't and you know it. I've got five thumbs and no finesse.
Barbara (*smiling*) Oh, Helen.
Helen It's true. I remember, when I was a kid, one of the farm hands saying to me—I'd just done something stupid or clumsy or both—and he said, "God help the man you marry, Miss Helen, you may be okay with cattle, but you'll be a disaster in the home."
Barbara Oh, what nonsense.
Helen He was right.
Barbara (*to Julie*) Don't start making yourself comfortable, Julie. Remember: homework first.
Julie Can't I even have a cup of tea?
Barbara Do you know what the time is? Your father will be home in a minute.
Helen Come on, Barbara, give the poor girl a cup of tea.
Barbara You spoil her. (*She gets up and goes to the kitchen*)
Helen Well, why not? (*To Julie*) Hey—I see the folk down the street are having a bonfire party tomorrow. Are you going?
Julie (*dismissively*) Oh no.

She gets up, picks up her satchel, coat, scarf, and gloves, crosses into the hall and into the kitchen, putting her things down on the chair at the table. Helen follows and sits at the table

Helen Too old for fireworks, huh?
Julie I've got better things to do.
Barbara Yes, she's got better things to do—like homework. (*To Julie*) Cake or biscuits?
Julie (*irritated*) Oh, Mum . . .! Neither, I *told* you.
Barbara (*to Helen*) Have you heard about this stupid diet?
Julie It's not stupid. Look at Sue Galleyford.
Barbara She's always been a big girl.

Julie Only because she eats so much.
Barbara Well, I think it's ridiculous—someone of your age . . .

The telephone rings

Julie I'll go—it's probably Maureen.
Barbara Hang your coat up! How many more times?
Julie Sorry, sorry. (*She picks up her raincoat and goes towards the hall*)
Barbara If it's that insurance man, tell him to ring back later.
Julie Okay. (*She closes the kitchen door. She hangs her raincoat on a peg and then answers the telephone*)
Barbara Would you like a cup of tea?
Helen No thanks, I'd better not.

Barbara makes tea for Julie

Say, whatever happened to the Pearsons?
Barbara The Pearsons . . .?
Helen Brian and Betty, down at number twenty-three.
Barbara They're all right, as far as I know.
Helen I've been round there half a dozen times and there's never anyone at home. I just wondered if they're okay.

Julie returns

Julie Who's that?
Helen The Pearsons.
Julie They've gone on holiday. (*To Barbara*) It's for you, Mum.
Helen (*to Julie*) At this time of the year?
Julie Only for a week. They're back tomorrow.

Barbara goes to the door

Barbara (*to Julie*) Who is it?
Julie A man.
Barbara What man?
Julie He didn't say.
Barbara Oh, Julie . . . (*She goes into the hall, closing the door. She goes to the telephone*)

Julie pours tea for herself

Julie Do you want some?
Helen No, thanks.

Julie sips her tea; Helen watches her

Well, now, young lady, and how are you today?
Julie Fine.
Helen Good.
Julie (*mock American accent*) Fine and dandy.
Helen Let's hope it stays that way.
Julie (*glancing at Helen*) Why shouldn't it?
Helen You tell me.

Julie turns, frowning, to face Helen

Julie What's the matter, Auntie Helen?
Helen I thought you weren't supposed to go riding about on motorcycles.
Julie Oh.
Helen Yes—oh.
Julie When did you see me?
Helen The other afternoon, with young Mr you-know-who.
Julie Malcolm.
Helen Yes, Malcolm. I thought all that was strictly *verboten*.
Julie He was only bringing me home from school—and he's very careful.
Helen Your momma doesn't think so.
Julie You know what she's like: she worries about everything.
Helen Only because she loves you.
Julie She keeps treating me like a little girl. She doesn't realize that I'm grown up.

Helen looks at Julie; she smiles affectionately

Helen No. No, and I don't suppose she ever will. (*She goes to Julie and kisses her*) Okay, I won't say a word. It'll be our secret. Don't do anything silly, do you hear me?
Julie (*smiling*) I won't. Thanks.

Barbara returns

Barbara Come on, Julie, what about that homework?
Julie (*to Helen, smiling*) See what I mean?
Barbara See what?
Julie Nothing. (*She picks up her cup of tea and goes to the door*) Who was that on the phone?
Barbara Someone for your father.

Julie slings her satchel over her shoulder

Julie Bye, Auntie Helen.
Helen Bye, sweetheart—work hard.
Julie I will.

Julie exits and goes upstairs

Helen She's a good girl.

Barbara finds Julie's gloves on a chair

Barbara If only she wasn't so untidy.

Helen has now changed back into her clothes

Helen There are worse things in life than being untidy.
Barbara You ought to try living with her. It takes at least half an hour to clear up the mess after she's gone to school: books and clothes all over the place—not to mention all the washing and ironing and mending. She doesn't do a thing for herself, it's disgraceful, really.
Helen Say what you like—she's a good girl and I'm very fond of her.

Barbara glances at Helen, mildly surprised by her uncharacteristically serious tone of voice

Barbara Yes—well, she's very fond of you.
Helen I hope so.
Barbara You know she is.
Helen I guess I do. (*She sighs*) I'd give a lot to have a daughter like Julie. You don't know how lucky you are.

Bob opens the front door. He is wearing a raincoat and a dark grey suit

Bob (*calling*) Hello.
Helen Hey, there's your old man. I must go.
Julie (*off*) Hello, Daddy!
Helen The dress is truly beautiful.
Barbara (*with a smile*) Thank you.

Helen goes to the hall. Bob is taking off his raincoat, which he hangs on a peg by the front door

Bob Ah—Helen.
Helen Don't look so worried, I'm just going. Is it still raining?
Bob It's raining, it's cold, and it's windy.
Helen Only one place to be on a night like tonight. Bed. Tucked up in bed, all cosy and warm, with the wind whistling outside. A little nooky, maybe. Poifeck, as my old Aunt Sophie used to say. (*Grinning at Barbara*) Hey. Maybe I'll call Malcolm Granger and see if he wants a few mind-broadening experiences. (*Calling upstairs*) Bye, honey. Bye, Bob. (*Blowing a kiss to Barbara*) Bye, sweetheart.
Julie (*off*) Bye.

Helen exits, closing the front door as she goes

Bob turns, smiling, to Barbara, who is standing by the kitchen door

Bob What's all that about Malcolm Granger?
Barbara Just a silly joke.

Barbara closes the kitchen door; she turns to face Bob; she is clearly anxious about something

Bob You all right?
Barbara Bob, listen—somebody's been ringing up for you—I think it's urgent.
Bob What is? Who?
Barbara His name's Stewart.
Bob Stewart what?
Barbara That's his surname—Mr Stewart.
Bob Who is he?
Barbara I don't know.
Bob What does he want?
Barbara I don't know.
Bob Didn't you ask him?

Barbara Of course I asked him! He said he wanted to talk to you. I told him you weren't here and could he ring back later, and he said no, he'd like to come and see us.

Bob What about?

Barbara I don't know—he got all cagey and said he couldn't explain on the phone.

Bob He's probably just a salesman.

Barbara No, he's something to do with the police.

Bob The police . . .?

Barbara He said if we were worried about him coming round here, we could ring Scotland Yard and speak to a Superintendent Smith.

Bob stares at her, but says nothing

And he said it's confidential; we mustn't tell anyone.

Momentarily at a loss for words, Bob walks aimlessly across the room

Bob When did he ring?

Barbara About five or ten minutes ago.

Bob Right . . . (*He goes to the door*) . . . Right, I'll talk to this man Smith. Where's his number?

Barbara It's on the pad.

Bob Right. (*He goes to the telephone and dials the number*)

Barbara remains by the kitchen door, observing

Barbara Ask him what it's all about.

Bob Yes, right. (*On the telephone*) Hello? . . . Hello, yes—could I speak to Superintendent Smith, please? My name's Jackson. (*Pause*) Hello? Is that Superintendent Smith? . . . Yes, good-evening—um—I understand a man called Stewart rang my wife just now and, um . . . Oh, did he? . . . Yes. . . . Yes. . . . Well, yes, of course, if it's important. . . . Yes. . . . Yes—um—can you tell me what it's all about? . . . Oh, I see. . . . Right. . . . Yes, I will. . . . Thank you, Superintendent. Goodbye.

Barbara Well?

Bob replaces the receiver. He turns to face Barbara

Bob Well, it's obviously pretty important.

Barbara What did he say?

Bob That's what he said. He said it's pretty important, and he'd be grateful if we could spare him the time to talk to this Mr Stewart.

A moment of silence. Barbara looks at Bob as if she had expected him to make more of a stand

He was very polite . . . very—you know, friendly and pleasant.

No response from Barbara

What else could I say?

Barbara What time is he coming?

Bob Eight o'clock.

Barbara I'd better get on with the supper, then.
Bob Right.

The Lights fade

Peter enters and addresses the audience

Peter I remember how shy they were when we first met. Helen and I went across and introduced ourselves: "Hi," we said, "we're your new neighbours." Well, Bob and Barbara stared at us as if we'd just stepped out of a flying saucer. They seemed a little reassured when we told them we were Canadians not Americans, but even so it took quite a time before they could accept us as regular human beings. A month or so later, they asked us to tea, and that's when we first met Julie. "Julie's short for Juliet," said Barbara, "Juliet as in *Romeo and Juliet*." Then Bob said, "We saw the old film with Norma Shearer and Leslie Howard just after we got engaged, and we made up our minds there and then: if we ever had a girl she was going to be called Juliet." "And so she was," said Barbara. "And so she was," said Bob. I was touched by the way they would finish each other's stories. It wasn't interrupting, it was more of a mutual orchestration of shared memories; a shared enjoyment of their life together. A kind of celebration. I said this to Helen when we got back home. She pooh-poohed it and said I was being sentimental; but pretty soon after she admitted that she too was beginning to feel a certain affection for them — Julie especially.

Peter exits

The Lights come up. Evening

Barbara and Bob are in the sitting-room, waiting anxiously for Mr Stewart to arrive. The curtains are drawn

A moment of silence

Barbara What's the time?
Bob Ten to.

Brief pause

Barbara I wish we knew what it was all about.
Bob Well, I did ask, didn't I? I couldn't do more than that.

Barbara sighs. Pause

Barbara I keep wondering if it's anything to do with Malcolm.
Bob Why should it be?
Barbara He's been in trouble with the police.
Bob What sort of trouble?
Barbara Something to do with his motorbike. Speeding, I think.
Bob I thought Julie wasn't seeing him anymore.
Barbara She still likes him.
Bob What's that supposed to mean?
Barbara What?

Bob Is she still seeing him or isn't she?
Barbara Well, I don't know. I can't be sure.
Bob Haven't you asked her?
Barbara Well, yes, but supposing she has seen him—and supposing——

The front doorbell rings. Barbara and Bob rise to their feet; they stand facing each other

Bob He's here.
Barbara He's early.

Bob turns to the door, but hesitates

Quickly! We don't want Julie to answer the door.

Bob goes into the hall. Barbara pats the cushions into shape. Bob opens the front door

Stewart enters. He is wearing a trilby hat, a raincoat, and a dark blue suit

Stewart Mr Jackson?
Bob Yes, that's right.
Stewart Good-evening, my name's Stewart. I spoke to your wife on the phone.
Bob Yes, do come in, please.
Stewart Thank you.

Stewart walks into the hall. Bob closes the front door and goes to the sitting-room

Bob This way.
Stewart Thank you.

Bob and Stewart enter the sitting-room

Bob This is my wife. Mr Stewart.
Stewart How do you do, Mrs Jackson.
Barbara How do you do.

They shake hands

Bob Let me take your coat.
Stewart Thank you. (*He takes off his raincoat; he gives it and his trilby hat to Bob*) Sorry I'm a bit early. I expected heavy traffic, but the roads were empty. It's all these gales, I suppose. People are staying at home.
Bob Yes. Yes, I suppose they are. (*He takes Stewart's raincoat and hat and hangs them in the hall*)
Stewart Dreadful floods in the south. Did you hear the news?
Barbara No, I . . .
Stewart Quite dreadful.

A brief, rather awkward silence. Bob returns

Barbara Please sit down, Mr Stewart.
Stewart Thank you.

Brief pause

Bob Now, then—what can we do for you?
Stewart Is your daughter at home?
Barbara Yes, she's upstairs—doing her homework.
Stewart I wonder, would it be possible to disturb her for a few minutes?
Bob Well, I ... (*an anxious hesitation*) ... do you have to see her?
Stewart I rather wanted to see you all, if that's possible—*en famille*, as it were.
Bob She's not in any trouble, is she?
Stewart Oh no, good Lord, no.
Barbara Well, that's a relief, anyway. (*She smiles*) I'll go and get her.
Stewart Thank you.

Barbara exits

Pause

Bob I spoke to Superintendent Smith.
Stewart Yes, so he said. (*A smile*) It's a bit melodramatic, I suppose, ringing Scotland Yard and all that, but—well, it's a good quick way of telling people that we're—you know—trustworthy, unlikely to run off with the family silver.

Stewart grins. Bob, too tense for light-hearted pleasantries, merely nods. Brief pause

I gather you're with AirSpeed Research?
Bob Yes.
Stewart That must be jolly interesting. Don't you find it interesting?
Bob Yes, oh yes, I enjoy it.
Stewart Travel about a bit, do you?
Bob Well not much; up and down to Liverpool mostly.
Stewart Ah. (*He smiles*) One tends to think of people in the aircraft industry as flying off all over the world at the drop of a hat.
Bob Not me, I'm afraid.
Stewart Pity.

Stewart smiles at Bob; there is another awkward silence before:

Barbara returns with Julie

Barbara This is our daughter, Julie, Mr Stewart.
Stewart How do you do, Miss Jackson.
Julie How do you do.

Stewart and Julie shake hands. Everyone sits down

Bob May I offer you a drink, sir? Whisky, sherry?
Stewart No, thanks, not for me, but please don't let me stop you.
Bob No ... no, I'm not much of a drinker.
Stewart Neither am I. Shockingly expensive these days.
Bob Yes, isn't it.

Stewart Shocking. (*Brief pause; he smiles*) Well, now, let me apologize for barging in on you like this. It's a bit alarming, I know, when a complete stranger rings up out of the blue, and I'm most grateful for you, ah—for your allowing me to come here—most grateful. The trouble is, it's a bit difficult for me to explain—precisely—what all this is about, what I do, and so on, because so much of my work concerns confidential matters, and I'm simply not allowed to discuss them in any detail.

Bob Fair enough.

Julie Are you a policeman?

Stewart Not really, no—although some of my duties—do tend to overlap with those of the police force. In actual fact, I'm a civil servant—(*he grins*) and that, as we all know, can cover a multitude of sins. (*He laughs; nobody responds to his joke; he rises to his feet*) Do you mind if I wander about? I find it so much easier to, um . . .

Barbara ⎱ (*together, giving their consent*) No, please.
Bob ⎰

Stewart Thank you (*He paces slowly across the room*) Now, then . . . the reason why I'm here. Well, we need your help, it's as simple as that. We've become very interested in one particular chap and we're anxious to find out what he does, where he goes, and so on. And the only way we can do that is by asking a lot of rather boring questions. In other words, it's just a straightforward, routine enquiry. There's nothing to be nervous about— it's just routine.

Bob Who is this man? Do we know him?

Barbara Does he live round here?

Stewart He comes here most weekends. We think he has friends in this part of the world.

The telephone rings

Bob Damn—sorry.

Stewart Not to worry.

Bob goes to answer the telephone

Bob (*on the telephone*) Hello? . . . Oh, Maureen—hang on a minute. . . . (*To Julie*) It's Maureen.

Julie Tell her I'll ring back later.

Bob (*on the telephone*) She says she'll ring back later. . . . What? . . . Right. . . . Yes, I'll tell her. . . . Yes, all right—bye-bye. (*He replaces the receiver and returns to the sitting-room*) She said she can't come round tomorrow evening.

Julie Why not?

Bob I don't know. Ring her later. (*To Stewart*) Sorry.

Stewart Not to worry. Um . . . where was I?

Julie You were saying about this man coming here to see his friends.

Stewart Ah yes. Now we don't know who they are or where exactly they live; we don't even know why he comes here so regularly. It might just be friendship, of course, but somehow I rather doubt it.

Julie Why?

Stewart He's a busy man, Miss Jackson, and if he takes the trouble to come out here every weekend, then I'm sure he does so for a very good reason. And that's why we think it's important to find out as much as we can about these weekly jaunts—and about these mysterious friends of his. Now—I've got a photograph of him somewhere ... (*He finds the photograph in his jacket pocket*) ... I'd like you all to take a look at it, if you will, and tell me if you think you've seen him before and if so, where.

Murmurs of assent

Mrs Jackson ...
Barbara (*looking at the photograph*) No, I've never seen him.
Stewart Mr Jackson?
Bob (*looking at the photograph*) No.
Stewart Miss Jackson.
Julie (*looking at the photograph*) No, sorry.
Stewart You're all quite sure?
Bob ⎫   ⎧Yes.
Barbara ⎬ (*together*)⎨ Quite sure.
Julie ⎭   ⎩Yes.
Stewart Yes, I see. Thank you. (*He puts the photograph back into his pocket*) Well, never mind, it was a long shot, anyway.
Julie What's he done, this man?
Stewart I'm afraid I can't tell you that, Miss Jackson.
Julie How do you know he comes here at weekends? Has somebody actually seen him?
Stewart Oh yes, we've been keeping an eye on him for some time.
Julie Do you mean following him?
Stewart (*smiling at her obvious excitement*) Well, yes, I suppose I do. But it's not as easy as it looks on the films, you know, following people— especially in a place like this, with all these narrow roads and footpaths. That's why I hoped that one of you might have seen him. It would have saved my chaps a lot of time and trouble.
Julie Would you like us to keep a look-out for him?
Stewart Yes, that would be splendid. (*Quickly adding a few words of restraint*) But do remember—you must remember that this is all very confidential. Not a word to anyone.
Bob Of course.
Stewart You do understand that, don't you, Miss Jackson? No whispering secrets to your chums at school.
Julie Yes, all right, I promise.
Stewart Good, excellent. Thank you.
Julie What happens next?
Barbara Ssshhh, Julie.
Stewart (*smiling*) That's a damn good question; I only wish I knew the answer.
Bob Well, if there's anything we can do ...
Stewart Thank you. (*He takes a notepad from his coat pocket*) As a matter of fact, there are one or two things I'd like to ask you before I go—just a

few details ... (*Opening the notepad*) You've lived here quite some time, I believe?

Bob Yes, over twenty years.

Stewart Really?

Bob Since March nineteen-thirty-nine.

Stewart My word. (*Taking a pen from his pocket*) So you'd know most of the other people here in Cranley Drive?

Bob My wife does, certainly.

Stewart Yes ... (*Turning to Barbara*) What about the Galleyfords at number thirty-eight? Do you know them?

Barbara Oh yes, they've been here almost as long as we have. Their daughter's the same age as Julie.

Stewart And they're English, I take it?

Barbara Yes—well, British—Mrs Galleyford comes from Cardiff.

Stewart Right. (*He makes a note*) Then there's the Duncans at number forty ...

Barbara He's retired—they're both in their seventies—they don't go out much.

Stewart (*making another note*) And across the road, at number forty-five— the Krogers.

Barbara Helen and Peter. They're our best friends, really. He's a bookseller.

Bob Book-dealer. Antiquarian books, you know, first editions.

Stewart Ah yes.

Bob They're Canadian.

Barbara But they're very nice. They've been here about five years.

Stewart Any family?

Barbara ⎫
Bob ⎭ (*together*) No.

Stewart (*making another note*) And next to them, at number forty-three ... (*Peering at his notes*) I can't read my own writing.

Barbara John and Sheila Henderson.

Stewart (*writing a correction*) Henderson ... yes.

Barbara They both go out to work, so I don't really know them. They moved in ... (*to Bob*) ... when?

Bob About a year ago.

Barbara A year ago, yes.

Stewart Right, good. (*Closing the notepad*) That's very useful. Thank you. (*He puts the notepad into his pocket and turns to Bob*) Now, you said you might be willing to help, Mr Jackson.

Bob Yes, of course.

Stewart Well, what we have to do is this. We have to station observers in various parts of the district and find out where this man goes, where he spends his Saturdays and Sundays. The problem is—how can our people observe without being observed? In Piccadilly at rush-hour, it couldn't be easier—but here, where everybody knows everybody else, it's really very difficult. The observer has to be concealed. There's no other way. (*A brief hesitation*) So that's what we need. A room. Somewhere. That's how you can help.

A moment of silence

Bob You mean a room *here* . . .?
Stewart It would only be for a couple of days: tomorrow and Sunday.

Barbara and Bob exchange anxious glances

Bob Well, I don't know about that . . .
Barbara You mean—one of your men—here, in the house?
Stewart It would be a young lady. More natural, we thought. If any questions are asked, you can say she's a member of your art club. It is an art club you belong to, isn't it?
Barbara (*amazed that he knows this*) Well, yes.

Stewart gestures to the paintings on the wall

Stewart Are these yours?
Barbara Yes.
Stewart Very good. Very good indeed. (*He smiles to Barbara, and then turns to Bob*) Well, what do you think? It seems to me that the smaller window upstairs at the front would probably be the best.
Julie (*excitedly*) That's my room!
Stewart (*smiling*) A good look-out post, eh, Miss Jackson?
Julie Oh yes—perfect.
Barbara I'm not too keen on having somebody actually inside the house.
Julie Why not?
Barbara Julie, please.
Stewart It's your decision. You must decide.
Bob Couldn't your people watch from a car—a parked car—couldn't they do that?
Stewart They *could*, yes—but not here. The roads are far too empty. An unfamiliar vehicle parked for any length of time would be painfully conspicuous. Don't you agree?
Bob (*reluctantly*) Well, yes . . .
Barbara Why don't you try Helen and Peter at number forty-five? They've got a much better view than we have.
Stewart I'm afraid we can't go from house to house trying to find the best view. Apart from anything else, we have to make sure that the people we go to are people we can trust—and it takes quite a bit of time to do that.
Bob To do what?
Stewart To make the necessary enquiries.
Bob You mean you've had us screened?
Stewart We checked. (*A small smile*) Better to be safe than sorry, after all. And since you're working on classified material at AirSpeed Research, we already knew something about you.

Brief pause, Bob is shaken to learn that he has been the subject of a security check; he looks at Barbara and then back to Stewart

Bob I see. So it's really important, then . . .?
Stewart We think it might be, yes.

Bob What about . . . I mean—would it be dangerous?

Stewart Dangerous . . .?

Bob Well, presumably this man's committed a crime of some sort.

Stewart He's not a thug, if that's what you mean. There's no danger of any physical violence.

Bob But he is a criminal . . .?

Stewart Let's say we have every reason to believe that he's involved in some kind of illegal activity.

Bob turns to Barbara

Bob What do you think?

Barbara It's up to you.

Bob hesitates for a moment; he then turns to Stewart and nods his approval

Bob All right, then. (*To Barbara*) All right?

Barbara (*with a nod*) All right.

Stewart (*smiling delightedly*) Thank you—thank you very much indeed. (*Turning to Barbara*) Would half-past nine tomorrow be convenient?

Barbara What for?

Stewart For my girl to arrive.

Barbara Oh yes . . . yes, that'll be fine.

Stewart I think it might be a good idea if she came in through the back garden, it's well hidden from the road and she could use the kitchen door, couldn't she? Would that be all right?

Barbara I suppose so.

Stewart Her name's Thelma by the way. I think you'll like her.

The Lights fade

Stewart exits

Thelma enters and addresses the audience: she is in her late twenties, a sturdily built ex-regular army girl; she wears a sweater and slacks

Thelma I noticed that everything had been tidied away; the furniture smelt of lavender polish and there was a vase of fresh flowers on the hall table; it was as if the house had been put on its best behaviour. I went upstairs, to the daughter's bedroom. There was a half-empty mug of coffee, still warm, on the bedside table. On the chest-of-drawers, a tin of Max Factor talcum powder stood beside a bottle of perfume, shaped like a cat. Holiday postcards from friends were stuck around the mirror. There was a portable gramophone and some records: Roy Orbison and the Everley Brothers. She was reading *Wuthering Heights*. I could hear the Jacksons moving and talking downstairs. They were talking quietly because there was a stranger in the house. (*Brief pause*) The day passed uneventfully, and when I left, at half-past five, Mrs Jackson asked me if I had been comfortable. I couldn't help smiling. Surveillance jobs usually mean spending hours, if not days, in cold empty rooms—or, worse, crouched in the back of a van. "Yes, thanks," I said, "very nice," I said, "very comfortable."

Thelma exits

The Lights come up. Evening

Barbara and Bob are seated in armchairs in the sitting-room. Barbara is sewing; Bob is reading a newspaper. The electric fire casts a cosy glow across the hearth. Pause. Bob yawns and turns a page of his newspaper

Barbara I wonder where he is?
Bob (*without looking up*) Who?
Barbara The man they're looking for.

No response; brief pause

I wonder what he's doing tonight? (*Pause; she raises her head and looks at Bob*) Perhaps he's married. Do you think he is?
Bob Stop worrying.
Barbara I'm not worrying.
Bob (*lightly*) You could've fooled me.

Pause

Barbara We don't know anything about him. Nothing. We don't even know what he's done.
Bob We don't need to.
Barbara Because of us he might be arrested. Just think of that. We ought to know something.

Bob lowers his newspaper

Bob Because of *us* . . .?
Barbara Because we let them watch.

Bob grins

Bob Trust you to say a thing like that.
Barbara Like what?
Bob Trust you to find a way of blaming yourself. Doesn't matter what it is, does it? If there's a hole in my sock, if the car breaks down—it's always your fault. Well, this isn't.

Barbara looks at him, but says nothing

So stop worrying.

Barbara nods her head, but her expression remains troubled and anxious

Do you fancy a cup of tea?
Barbara Do you?
Bob I don't mind.
Barbara A bit later, then.
Bob Right. (*He stands up, stretches, strolls to the window, and draws the curtains. He glances across the road*) It looks as if Helen and Peter are having an early night. Off for a bit of—what does she call it?—off for a bit of nooky.

Barbara smiles, but remains silent. Bob goes back to his chair

I just can't imagine it, can you?

Barbara What?

Bob All these wild nights we hear so much about. I can't imagine them actually performing.

Barbara Oh, I don't know. Peter's quite attractive.

Bob glances at Barbara, mildly surprised

Bob Is he?

Barbara Well, not unattractive.

Bob grins

Bob God, the idea of waking up alongside Dizzy Lizzie—the mind boggles!

Barbara smiles. Bob resumes reading his newspaper; Barbara sews; a clock strikes the half-hour; Bob turns a page of his newspaper

Barbara Do you remember that time we saw a man being arrested outside the bus station?

Bob What man?

Barbara Don't you remember?

Bob Who . . .?

Barbara We were going somewhere, the three of us—Julie was quite small—and we saw these policemen running into the bus station. Then they grabbed a man and took him away. Don't you remember? His clothes were all stained and dirty. I thought he was old at first, an old tramp or something, but then he walked past I could see he was young— younger than me. And he was crying. Don't you remember? I thought it was so sad. He wasn't just crying, he was sobbing. It was awful.

Bob stares at Barbara; there is a moment of silence before he speaks

Bob What am I supposed to say to that?

Barbara I don't know.

Bob What?

Barbara (*shrugging*) Nothing.

Bob He might have bashed some old lady over the head and pinched her handbag. Supposing he had. How would you feel about him then?

Barbara People don't stop being people just because they've done something wrong. They still have feelings.

Bob (*firmly*) Look—it's nothing to do with us, none of it. Mr Stewart says this man's mixed up with something criminal, something illegal—well, that's all we need to know. Who he is and what he's done just doesn't matter. It's none of our business.

No response

Well, is it?

Barbara I don't know.

Bob Well, it isn't. Take it from me. (*Again he opens his newspaper*)

Barbara sews; pause

Is it the same girl coming back tomorrow?
Barbara Yes.
Bob Thelma.
Barbara Thelma, yes.
Bob She seems quite nice. (*He turns a page of his newspaper*) Must be a bit boring, sitting upstairs all day. (*He glances at Barbara*) Still, just think; this time tomorrow, it'll all be over. She'll have gone.

The Lights fade

Barbara walks downstage and addresses the audience

During the following, Stewart enters the sitting-room

Barbara Sunday—a really beautiful morning, almost summery, not a cloud in the sky. It must have been about eleven o'clock when Bob and Julie went out to wash a car—well, not quite eleven, the church bells were still ringing. I love the sound of church bells on Sunday mornings. I'd got a shoulder of lamb for lunch and I'd just finished doing the vegetables when Thelma came down for a cup of coffee. We went into the sitting-room and stood there, by the window. I thought how friendly she was—not at all what I imagined a police girl would be like. Then Julie came in for some clean water and told us about her friend Maureen Chapman—apparently there'd been some sort of domestic disaster; she'd let the bath overflow and the hall ceiling needed redecorating—Julie asked if she could go round after lunch and help, and of course I said yes. Thelma and I were both talking, laughing, saying what a mess it must have been, when Thelma suddenly looked out of the window. I looked out too, I don't know why, I just did. Helen's front door was open and somebody was coming out of the house. It was a man. I'd never seen him before. He didn't look round to say goodbye, he just hurried to the gate and went off along the road. He had disappeared before I realized who it was. Thelma turned to me and said, "Did you see what I saw?" I couldn't speak. I just nodded. It was the man in the photograph, the man Mr Stewart was looking for. Thelma went to make a phone call. I just stood there, by the window. I could hear Julie laughing and talking as she cleaned the car. The church bells were still ringing. Although I didn't know what it meant, I felt sure something terrible had happened. Then Thelma came back. "Mr Stewart's coming to see you this afternoon," she said, "it's very important. Don't tell Julie." (*Brief pause*) Somehow I forced myself to eat some lunch. The meat kept turning and turning in my mouth. I couldn't swallow. When Julie went off to paint Maureen's ceiling, I told Bob what had happened. He gave me a hug. "Don't worry," he said, "there's nothing to worry about." But as he held me in his arms, I could feel his hands trembling.

The Lights come up. Afternoon

Barbara walks directly into the sitting-room, where Bob and Stewart are awaiting

Stewart You actually saw this man yourself, Mrs Jackson?

Barbara Yes, I did.

Stewart You saw him come out of number forty-five Cranley Drive and hurry away along the road?

Barbara Yes.

Stewart And you're quite sure it was the same man—the man whose photograph I showed you?

Barbara Yes, oh yes.

Stewart Yes, I see. (*He turns to Bob*) Well, it seems you missed all the excitement, Mr Jackson. You were cleaning your car, I believe?

Bob Yes.

Stewart Just here, in front of your house?

Bob Yes.

Stewart Yes, well . . . you can see how easy it is for him to come and go without being observed. Amazing isn't it?

No response

He must have arrived in Ruislip yesterday lunchtime; that's when his car was seen, anyway. Saturday lunchtime to Sunday morning. Presumably to spend the night with these friends of yours. (*Brief pause; he turns to Bob*) Have you told your daughter any of this?

Bob No.

Stewart Good, that's probably just as well. Don't tell her—for the time being, at any rate. Where is she?

Barbara Out with some friends.

Stewart Oh good. (*He takes a cigarette pack from his jacket pocket*) Do you mind if I . . .?

Bob No no, please do.

Stewart Thank you. Well, what a surprise. It must have been quite a surprise for you, Mrs Jackson; something of a bolt out of the blue, I should imagine.

No response

He was on his way to fetch his car when you saw him. He always parks it in the same place: outside that block of flats—what's it called? That block of flats in the next street.

Barbara Ruislip Court.

Stewart Yes, Ruislip Court. He always parks it there. It's an unusual car, you may have seen it: a white Studebaker Farina, licence number ULA six-one. Does that ring any bells?

Barbara shakes her head

Bob No, sorry.

Stewart No, well, never mind. (*A small smile*) I can't imagine why he chose a flashy job like that; singularly inappropriate in his line of business.

Bob What is that?

Stewart What?

Bob What is his line of business?

Stewart hesitates

Can't you tell us what he's done?

Stewart Well, we're not entirely sure. We think he may have entered the country illegally.

Pause

Barbara What does that mean?

Stewart What?

Barbara I don't understand what you mean.

Stewart We think he may have entered this country with a false passport and under an assumed name, Gordon Lonsdale.

Brief pause; Barbara and Bob are both looking at Stewart, clearly waiting for him to say more

It's difficult to be absolutely sure. We'll need to make a few more enquiries. It's early days yet.

Barbara Yes, but what's he actually done? Why won't you tell us?

Stewart turns and looks directly at Barbara

Stewart We think he may be working—covertly—for a foreign government.

Bob Covertly . . .?

Stewart Secretly.

Bob You mean he's a spy . . .?

Stewart Well, something of that sort—but I'd rather not jump to conclusions until we know a little more.

Bob (*almost laughing*) But what would a spy be doing in Peter's home?

Stewart Well, quite . . .

Bob There must be some mistake.

Barbara Shouldn't we tell them? Shouldn't we warn them?

Stewart All in good time, Mrs Jackson.

Bob Oh, come on, you're not suggesting that they're involved with this man, are you?

Stewart responds with an ambiguous shrug

Barbara Oh no—not Helen and Peter—they wouldn't do a thing like that.

Stewart Maybe not.

Barbara But we've known them for years, Mr Stewart—five years!

Stewart Yes, so you said.

Barbara Oh, but look . . . how can you even think such a thing? He must be just a casual friend.

Bob A business friend.

Barbara Yes, another bookseller—something like that.

Stewart Well, possibly.

Silence. Bob rises to his feet

Bob I think I'll have a drink. Barbara? Sir?

She shakes her head

Stewart No, thank you.

Bob pours a neat scotch for himself. Pause

So your friends have never spoken about this Mr Lonsdale?
Bob No, never.
Barbara Never.
Stewart That's a bit strange, don't you think?
Bob Why strange?
Stewart A man who comes to see them almost every weekend ... you'd have thought they would have mentioned his name at the very least. (*Brief pause*) Wouldn't you have thought so, Mrs Jackson?
Barbara I don't know ...
Stewart You may be right, of course, he may be just a casual friend, but he's not a bookseller—that's for sure. He's director of a firm called Allo Security Products Limited; they make antiburglar devices for cars. A bit of a man-about-town, too—ritzy flat near Regent's Park, plenty of girlfriends—not at all the sort you'd expect to get pally with the Krogers.

Barbara stares at Stewart; vague suspicions are beginning to form in her mind

Barbara You seem to know an awful lot about him.
Stewart Not enough, alas.
Barbara Are you sure you didn't know where to find him?
Stewart (*glancing sharply at Barbara*) How do you mean?
Barbara It seems very lucky choosing our house. Right opposite Helen and Peter's. I mean—that seems almost too good to be true.
Stewart (*with an easy smile*) These things do happen, Mrs Jackson. We all deserve a little luck from time to time.

Barbara makes no response. Stewart strolls across the room and sits facing her

At the risk of sounding rather unfriendly, it's my duty to draw your attention to the Official Secrets Act. We're all bound by it, you know, as we're bound by any other law. I'd intended to bring the Declaration along for you both to sign—but what with one thing and another, I quite forgot. Not that it matters really. The signing of the Act is just a way, the customary way, of reminding you of its existence and its importance. (*A smile*) Legal red tape. And we get plenty of that in my job, I can tell you. (*Brief pause*) All we're asking for is discretion; sensible, reasonable discretion. All right?

Barbara and Bob nod their heads. Stewart grins and rises to his feet

Good! Well, now ... tell me about the Krogers.
Bob Tell you what?
Stewart Anything. What sort of people are they?
Bob They're damn good neighbours.
Stewart Yes, but what do you know about them? Where did they live before they came here?
Bob South London. Catford, I think.

Stewart And you said they're Canadians . . .?

Barbara Yes.

Stewart Canadians—not Americans?

Barbara Oh no—Helen's most particular about that. I remember once somebody introduced them as an American couple and Helen got really angry: "Canadian," she said, "not American—Canadian!" She almost shouted it.

Stewart Whereabouts in Canada do they come from? Do you know?

Bob No.

Stewart No idea at all?

Bob Helen was brought up in the country somewhere.

Barbara She's always telling Julie stories about her life on the farm.

Stewart What sort of stories?

Bob How she could climb trees better than any of the boys.

Barbara Chop wood.

Bob Ride horses, that sort of thing, you know.

Stewart (*smiling*) So she was a real tom-boy.

Barbara (*also smiling*) She still is. Mind you, I'm never quite sure how much of it to believe.

Stewart Ah.

The smile fades from Barbara's face as she realizes the possible significance of her last remark

Barbara Well . . . they're just stories she tells Julie. She probably exaggerates a bit.

Stewart Yes. (*Brief pause*) What about Peter Kroger? What sort of a person is he?

Bob Very different from Helen.

Barbara Completely different.

Bob A marriage of opposites, we always say.

Barbara He's very quiet. Bookish, you know.

Bob Intellectual.

Barbara Yes, he's an intellectual.

Stewart And where's his bookshop—in London?

Bob He used to have a shop in the Strand, but now it's a mail-order business. He sends out lists and works from home.

Stewart Uh-huh. And you'd say that they're happy—it's a happy marriage?

Bob Oh, very.

Barbara Very happy.

Stewart Yes, I see.

Barbara bows her head, fighting back tears

Barbara I do hate talking about them like this.

Stewart Yes, I'm sorry. It's a most unpleasant situation, I know. Rotten luck.

Pause. Bob rests a comforting hand on Barbara's shoulder

Bob What happens now?

Stewart Well, obviously it's in everybody's best interest to get to the bottom
of, uh ... well, whatever's going on. We have to find out what this fellow
Lonsdale's up to. That's very important.

Bob Yes.

Stewart Crucially important.

Bob Yes.

Stewart Likewise your friends, the Krogers: are they involved with him or
are they not? (*Brief pause*) All of which means, alas, that we'll have to
trespass upon your hospitality for just a few more days.

Barbara (*her head jerks up*) What?

Stewart The point is this: We think Lonsdale may be in a spot of trouble.
He's had a few business problems just recently—money problems—and
this could make him do something rash, reckless. If he does, we want to
know about it. And that means keeping an eye on things. And that means
somebody here in this house—as from tomorrow, if that's possible.

Barbara (*aghast*) You mean——

Bob (*overlapping*) Tomorrow? Why tomorrow? I thought he only came here
at weekends.

Stewart We can't be sure. Things might change.

Barbara You mean you want to keep somebody here every day?

Stewart Just for a week or so.

Barbara (*incredulous*) Every day ...?

Stewart Well, yes.

Barbara Oh, but you can't expect us to do that—it's out of the question.

Stewart We'd disturb you as little as possible——

Barbara No, I'm sorry.

Stewart —and I wouldn't ask if it wasn't really necessary.

Bob Yes, but look——

Barbara What about Julie? What about her homework?

Bob Yes.

Stewart No problem there. It gets dark at—what?—four-thirty, five—no
point us staying after that.

Barbara Yes, but think how she'll *feel*; she'll be so upset.

Stewart Upset ...?

Barbara Because of Helen and Peter; she's very fond of them.

Bob She loves them.

Barbara She does.

Stewart Well, there's no need to worry her with any of this.

Bob We'll have to tell her something.

Stewart Say it's just a routine investigation—there's no need to go into
details.

Barbara She won't believe that.

Stewart Why not? Children accept things very easily.

Barbara She's not a child.

Bob There must be an easier way of finding out.

Stewart I only wish there were.

Bob Why don't you just go across and ask them?

Stewart You mean the Krogers?

Bob Yes.

Stewart Ask them what?

Bob Ask them what they know about this man—what he was doing there this morning.

Stewart Supposing they're involved with him in some way?

Barbara Oh, but they're not. I know they're not.

Stewart Supposing they are . . .

Barbara They're not.

Stewart Just suppose. We can't afford to take the risk. (*Brief pause*) Well, can we?

Barbara You've obviously decided what you're going to do, so why bother to ask us?

Stewart Try to look at it from my point of view, Mrs Jackson. Lonsdale was seen coming out of their house. That's bound to create a certain amount of suspicion. It's bound to. We can't ignore it. We can't pretend it never happened. We have to act accordingly. We have to.

Pause

Bob So what are you saying? What are you suggesting?

Stewart Only that the present arrangement should continue . . . for a week or so. That's all. Nothing more.

Barbara I don't think you understand, Mr Stewart. Helen and Peter are our best friends. We see them every day.

Stewart Yes, I know.

Barbara Helen, especially. She's always popping in.

Stewart Yes, I know.

Barbara Well, you can't expect me to talk to her and have cups of tea with her when I know there's somebody spying on her from Julie's bedroom. I can't do that. I can't. Well, I won't. I'm sorry.

Stewart Perhaps you could try . . . just for a day or two.

Barbara Why should I?

Always the peacemaker, Bob recognizes a bellicose tone in Barbara's voice; he turns pacifically to Stewart

Bob It's asking a hell of a lot, you know.

Stewart (*quietly*) I'm afraid I must insist.

Bob *Insist* . . .?

Stewart Earnestly implore.

Barbara Oh, it's just not fair, Mr Stewart.

Stewart It's not, I agree—but being fair has a pretty low priority at the moment. (*Pause*) I really am very sorry.

Pause

Bob Would it be the same girl?

Stewart Well, yes, I thought so. There might have to be another one—just to give Thelma a bit of a rest. It can be quite tiring, you know, peering out of a window all day long. You'd be surprised. We'll have a separate

telephone line installed upstairs. No bell, of course, just a little red light—
so it shouldn't be too irksome for you.

Bob takes a deep breath; he turns to Barbara

Bob What do you think?
Barbara (*tersely*) You know what I think.

Bob sighs. Brief pause

Bob Well, if it's only a week ... (*He nods his head, giving reluctant consent*)
Stewart Thank you, Mr Jackson. (*He turns to Barbara*) I find this part of
my job very painful and unpleasant. Unfortunately—it has to be done.
Barbara You're wrong about Helen and Peter. It's nothing to do with them.
Stewart Time alone will tell.
Barbara They've been such good friends, such close friends ...
Stewart And you think you'd have guessed?
Barbara We'd have guessed something—instinctively.
Stewart Mrs Jackson, people like Lonsdale and his colleagues spend their
lives deceiving people like you. It's their job, their profession, and they do
it with the utmost skill and conviction. If they didn't, they'd be finished.

*The front door opens and Julie enters. She is wearing a raincoat over her
paint-spattered sweater and slacks*

Julie (*calling as she enters*) Mum!
Bob In here, Julie.

Julie takes off her raincoat as she enters the sitting-room

Julie Oh, hello, Mr Stewart.

Stewart rises to his feet

Barbara (*before Stewart has a chance to respond*) You're covered in paint!
Covered!
Julie I know, I know. I'm going to have a bath. (*To Stewart*) I've been
painting a ceiling and it kept dripping down. (*Turning to leave*) Any sign
of that man?
Bob (*hastily interposing*) Julie, listen—there's been a change of plan.
Thelma's not going after all.
Julie Oh good.
Stewart She'll only be here in the daytime, of course—so perhaps you
wouldn't mind if she invaded your bedroom again?
Julie No, that's fine.
Bob And you mustn't tell anyone.
Julie I know.
Bob It's important, Julie—not anyone.
Julie I know! (*Smiling at Stewart*) Don't worry, Mr Stewart, I won't
breathe a word.
Stewart (*with a smile*) No, I'm sure you won't.
Julie Bye, then.

Julie exits and goes upstairs

Pause

Stewart Well, there's nothing more to say, is there? (*Turning to Bob*) If you have any problems, just telephone Superintendent Smith at Scotland Yard.

Bob Right.

Stewart turns to Barbara

Stewart Thank you again, Mrs Jackson. I'll do everything I can to make our presence here as unobtrusive as possible.

Stewart goes to the hall; Bob follows. Barbara remains motionless for a moment; she then walks across the room and draws the curtains. She switches on the light. Bob and Stewart are shaking hands in the hall

Stewart goes out

Bob closes the front door and returns to the sitting-room; Barbara turns and glares at him

Bob Don't blame me.

Barbara I don't want those people here. I don't want them in the house!

Bob Be reasonable. There was nothing I could do.

Barbara You could have said no, couldn't you?

Bob Well, hardly.

Barbara You're always the same with people like that.

Bob Like what?

Barbara You know what I mean—like a schoolboy in front of the head-master.

Bob Look, there's no point in——

Barbara I just don't want to talk about it, Bob. I don't want anything to do with it! (*She turns from him and paces across the room*) What about Julie?

Bob What about her?

Barbara What are we going to say to her?

Bob Well, nothing—I mean . . .

Barbara What?

Bob Well . . .

Barbara Doesn't it worry you that we're deceiving her like this?

Bob We're not deceiving her.

Barbara We're not telling her the truth. You heard him tell us just how, "Don't tell Julie". Doesn't that make you feel *sick*?

Pause. Barbara and Bob stand facing each other

Bob Look—there was nothing we could do.

Barbara Of course there was.

Bob We couldn't say no.

Barbara Why not?

Bob Well, suppose he's right . . .

Barbara Right about what?

Bob Helen and Peter knowing this man.

Barbara Oh, for heaven's sake . . .!

Bob It's possible—I mean it's possible.

Barbara Don't be ridiculous.

Bob You just think about it.

Barbara Don't be ridiculous.

Bob When have we ever seen them on a Saturday or Sunday? When? You just think about it.

Barbara Dozens of times.

Bob Not once.

Barbara What about that trip to the zoo?

Bob What trip?

Barbara When was it? Two or three months ago.

Bob That was August Bank Holiday Monday. We never see them at weekends—never.

Barbara Of course we do.

Bob Never.

Barbara Oh, that's just——

Bob What?

Barbara Nonsense.

Bob Is it?

Barbara You know it is.

The telephone rings. Bob turns from Barbara; he goes to the hall and answers the telephone

Bob (*on the telephone*) Hello? . . . Oh, hello, Maureen—just a minute. . . . (*He calls upstairs*) Julie! It's for you!

Julie (*off*) Who is it?

Bob Maureen.

Julie (*off*) I'm getting changed. I'll ring back later.

Bob (*on the telephone*) Did you hear that? She'll ring later. . . . Right. . . . Yes, all right—bye-bye. (*He replaces the receiver. He returns to the sitting-room*)

Barbara has not moved. They stand facing each other

Shall I ring up and say we've changed our minds? I'll ring that man at Scotland Yard, shall I? Would you like me to do that? Shall I?

Barbara It's too late.

Bob Why? Why, what do you mean?

Barbara You know what I mean. (*She walks past him and goes to the kitchen*)

The Lights fade

Bob exits. Barbara exits through the back door

The Lights come up. Day. Music from the kitchen radio

Barbara enters from the garden, carrying some vegetables. She is wearing an apron

The front doorbell rings. Barbara reacts with a degree of alarm. She puts the vegetables on the kitchen table and switches off the radio. The doorbell rings again. Barbara goes quietly, almost on tip-toe, to the sitting-room. She peers round the edge of the curtains. She springs back. She stands tense and motionless by the window. The doorbell rings again. Barbara can delay no longer; she walks to the hall and opens the front door

Helen enters; she is wearing outdoor clothes and carries a shopping basket. Peter follows behind

Helen Jesus, you were a long time.
Barbara Sorry, sorry.
Helen We thought you must be out.
Barbara No, I . . .
Helen Weren't in the john, were you?
Barbara No . . .
Helen (*as she walks to the sitting-room*) If there's one thing I hate, it's being hauled out of the john in the middle of it.

Barbara closes the front door

Peter How are you, Barbara?
Barbara I'm just about to do some painting.
Peter We're not staying, don't worry. We're just——
Helen (*overlapping*) We're going up to town. Is there anything you want? (*She catches sight of the easel*) Hey—how's the easel?
Barbara What?
Helen The easel—is it okay?
Barbara Oh yes. Yes, it's fine.
Helen If it's not, you just say and I'll take it back.
Barbara No, it's fine, I love it.
Helen The guy in the store said he'd change it if you didn't like it.
Peter (*to Helen*) She says it's fine, she loves it, what more can she say? (*Going to the door*) Come on, let's leave the girl in peace.
Helen What's the hurry?
Peter The whole idea was to get up to town before the crowds, remember?
Helen Okay, okay.
Peter (*to Barbara*) We're making an early start on the Christmas shopping. Helen's got a list a mile long (*To Helen*) Show her.
Helen Show her . . .?
Peter Show her the list.
Helen You've got it. I gave it to you.
Peter You didn't.
Helen In the kitchen—you were putting your coat on.
Peter You put it in your purse.
Helen I did what?
Peter Didn't you?
Helen (*suddenly remembering*) I left it on the kitchen table—Jesus!
Peter Are you sure?
Helen Sure I'm sure—it's on the goddam table.

Peter (*grinning*) Okay, I'll go get it. (*To Helen, as he goes to the hall*) And I
   want you outside, in the car, ready to go, in five minutes—okay?
Helen Okay.
Peter (*to Barbara*) Take care of yourself, Barbara.
Barbara You too.

Peter exits

Helen Just imagine going up to town and forgetting your goddam shopping
   list! Jeeze, I must be going out of my mind.

*Barbara, ill-at-ease, manages a small smile. Helen watches as Barbara
prepares to start painting.*

So who's the mystery man, huh? And don't pretend you don't know what
   I'm talking about.
Barbara What?
Helen Yesterday afternoon—about four o'clock—I saw some guy walking
   across the street. It looked like he was coming from here.
Barbara Well, yes, he was.
Helen Aha! It's lucky I knew your old man was at home, otherwise I might
   have gotten very suspicious indeed. Who is he?
Barbara Oh—just a friend of Bob's.
Helen Yeah, I thought so. Didn't I see him at your wedding anniversary?
Barbara No, that was somebody else.
Helen Are you sure?
Barbara Quite sure.
Helen Gee, that's funny. I could have sworn he was the guy Bob introduced
   me to. What's his name?
Barbara Um ... Stewart.
Helen Stewart?
Barbara He's never been here before, so you can't have met him.
Helen Okay, if you say so. (*She strolls to the door*) Now, look, about this
   Christmas shopping—what do you think Julie would like?
Barbara Oh, look, you mustn't bother ...
Helen What do you mean—bother? It's no bother. I love buying her
   presents. It gives me pleasure. She's always so appreciative. I was
   wondering about a blouse. Do you think she'd like that? A silk blouse.
Barbara Well, yes, that would be lovely, but you mustn't be too extrava-
   gant.
Helen Why not, for heaven's sake? There's nothing I enjoy more than real
   sinful extravagance. (*She winks playfully*) Born to be bad, that's me. (*She
   kisses Barbara on the cheek*) I'd better go, I'll see you later, honey. (*Going
   to the door*) Do you want anything from the shops?
Barbara (*suddenly, impulsively*) Helen ...

Helen pauses, looking back at Barbara

We're thinking of having a few friends in for a drink on Saturday evening.
   Would you and Peter like to come?
Helen Oh, we can't this Saturday. What a shame.

Barbara Well, we'll change it. We'll make it next Saturday. Saturday week.

Helen Saturday's always difficult for us. I'd better say no. Peter likes to do his accounts at the weekend. You know that. We told you. (*She smiles*) Thanks for asking. *Ciao!*

Helen exits

Barbara remains motionless

CURTAIN

ACT II

The Lights come up. Day

The back door opens and Thelma enters from the garden; she is wearing a crash helmet, goggles, a waterproof cape, and leggings

Thelma Mrs Jackson? It's me. Sally?

Sally walks down the stairs. She is about thirty; pleasant, but rather plain; middle-class. She wears a sweater, skirt and raincoat; she is carrying an umbrella. She goes to the kitchen

Sally You're late.

Thelma I know, sorry. There's been an accident on the Western Avenue and the traffic's murder. (*She takes off her motorcycling gear*) What about that rain—did you see it? I really thought the end of the world had come.

Sally That motorbike of yours makes a hell of a noise. Are you sure Mr Stewart said you could bring it?

Thelma Of course—why not? There are dozens of motorbikes around here. You don't think the Krogers are going to notice one extra, do you? (*Looking around*) Where's Mrs Jackson?

Sally Out shopping.

Thelma Poor thing. I hope she didn't get caught in that storm. (*She drapes her cape and leggings over a chair*) God, I'm dying for a cup of tea. How about you?

Sally No, thanks. I've just had one.

Thelma goes to the sink and fills the electric kettle

Thelma Look, don't worry—I always park the bike round the corner. I park it somewhere different every day—and never outside the house. (*Switching on the kettle*) So what's been happening this morning?

Sally Nothing much—just routine comings and goings.

Thelma As per usual. (*She yawns*) It's going to be a long job, this one.

Sally Do you think so?

Thelma Don't you?

Sally (*shrugging*) I don't know.

Thelma Oh yes—this is a biggie. I can smell it. (*Spooning tea into the pot*) Mr Stewart went to the American Embassy yesterday—twice.

Sally How do you know?

Thelma Sylvia told me. She went out with Bill last night. He was duty driver yesterday, and he told her. Twice in a day! That must mean it's a biggie.

Thelma takes a bottle of milk from the fridge and puts it on the table

Sally Don't leave the milk there. You'll have Mrs Jackson tut-tutting at you.

Thelma (*not understanding*) Why?

Sally She always puts milk in a jug, haven't you noticed? She obviously thinks milk in bottles is common.

Thelma makes no response; she takes the jug from a cupboard and pours the milk into it. Sally watches

Can you imagine what her life must be like? Dusting and washing and ironing and polishing and cooking. God. No wonder she's as dull as she is.

Thelma I like her.

Sally looks at her

Sally Yes, you do, don't you? (*She buttons her raincoat*) She thinks we're going at the end of the week.

Thelma Did she say so?

Sally Sort of. She keeps dropping hints.

Thelma Like what?

Sally "It'll seem strange without you next week", that sort of thing, you know.

Thelma What did you say?

Sally Well, nothing. What could I say?

Thelma sighs, but says nothing; she is standing by the window, waiting for the kettle to boil

Right, then—I'll be off.

Thelma Right.

Sally goes to the back door

Clark Gable died.

Sally Yes, I heard it on the radio.

Thelma I think it's really sad, don't you? No more Clark Gable. Gone forever.

The front door opens. Sally and Thelma swing round, suddenly alert

Barbara enters; she is wearing a raincoat and carrying shopping bags

Mrs Jackson?

Barbara (*closing the front door*) Hello. What a dreadful morning! Did you see that rain?

Sally Wasn't it awful?

Thelma I thought the end of the world had come. (*She makes the tea*)

Sally At least you didn't get too wet.

Barbara No, I was lucky. Pour me a cup, would you, Thelma? (*Putting the shopping bags on the table*) Those bags weigh a ton.

Sally Is it raining now?

Barbara Not really—but there's more on the way, by the look of it.

Sally I'd better go. (*To Thelma, as she goes to the back door*) I'll see you tomorrow.

Thelma It's Pat tomorrow—I don't come back till Saturday.

Sally Okay, I'll see you then. Bye, Mrs Jackson.

Barbara Bye, Sally.

Thelma Bye.

Sally exits

Barbara She's a nice girl.

Thelma (*pouring the tea*) Milk and two sugars?

Barbara Yes, please. (*She starts to unload the shopping*) I got some sausages for lunch. Do you like sausages?

Thelma I love them—but you really must stop cooking all these meals for us.

Barbara I'd hardly call sausages a meal.

Thelma Mr Stewart would be furious if he knew.

Barbara Don't tell him, then.

Thelma (*grinning*) Don't worry, I won't.

Barbara takes some tins of food to the store cupboard

(*Giving a cup of tea to Barbara*) Here ...

Barbara Thanks.

Barbara and Thelma sip their tea. Pause

Thelma Clark Gable died, did you know?

Barbara Yes. What was it—a heart attack or something?

Thelma Yes, I think so. Sad isn't it. (*Pause*) Mind you, he wasn't as good as Gregory Peck. Or Richard Burton. I think he's wonderful. Did you see him on TV the other night?

Barbara No.

Thelma He was wonderful. Those eyes. That voice.

The front doorbell rings

Silently, furtively, Thelma gathers her motorcycling gear and hurries upstairs

Barbara waits, tense, until the coast is clear. Then she goes to the front door and opens it

Helen enters

Helen Hi, honey, how are you?

Barbara Helen ...

Helen I've brought this tin back. (*She displays the cake-tin she is carrying, and walks to the kitchen*)

Barbara Oh yes ... thanks. (*She closes the front door and follows Helen*)

Helen Those little coookies were deelicious, Barbara. So light and crisp— yummy! How do you do it?

Barbara Oh—just a knack.

Helen Some knack. (*She turns, smiling, to Barbara*) So how's life? Is everything okay?

Barbara Yes, fine.

Helen How's Julie? I haven't seen her for ages.

Barbara She's fine—um ... working hard.

Helen Come to that, I haven't seen you either. You gave me those cookies on Monday, and here we are—it's Thursday. (*Mock-accusingly*) Have you been avoiding me, Barbara?

Barbara (*a stab of alarm*) Have I what?

Helen A joke, dear—I was joking.

Barbara Sorry, I didn't hear what you said.

Helen You're not mad at me, are you?

Barbara What?

Helen Well, are you?

Barbara No no, of course not. I've been a bit busy, that's all.

Helen Busy doing what?

Barbara Oh, nothing much.

Helen Busy doing nothing much ...?

Barbara Well, you know how it is.

Helen (*lightly*) No, I don't. I'm beginning to feel like the girl in the bad breath commercial. (*She smiles*)

No response from Barbara

How's the dress coming along?

Barbara The dress ...?

Helen My party dress.

Barbara Almost finished. Ready next week.

Helen Terrific! (*Glancing at the empty cups on the table*) Hey, what's all this?

Barbara What's all what?

Helen Two cups of tea on the kitchen table. Don't tell me you've got a lover hiding away upstairs.

Barbara Oh dear—fancy that. I haven't even washed up yet. (*Quickly plunging the cups into the sink*) Isn't that awful?

Helen (*staring at Barbara*) Are you sure you're all right, honey? You look kinda pale.

Barbara No, it's nothing, just a headache.

Helen Take a pill.

Barbara I have.

Helen Take another pill.

Barbara Yes, all right.

Helen I'll go get you one, shall I?

Barbara No, please ...

Helen You know me: pills and potions keep me going. I'll run upstairs and see what you've got.

Barbara It's all right, Helen. Please don't fuss!

Helen frowns, startled by Barbara's irritability

Helen Fuss ...?

Barbara I'm sorry, I'm sorry. I didn't mean to be rude.
Helen You be just as rude as you like, honey. I mean, jeeze, if you can't shout at friends, who can you shout at?
Barbara I didn't mean to shout. I'm sorry.

Helen goes to Barbara and takes her by the hand

Helen Look, I'll tell you what. Why don't you put your feet up, go to bed—read a book or something, huh?
Barbara Yes, perhaps I will.
Helen It'll only make things worse if you try to keep going.
Barbara Yes.
Helen How about some magazines ... Would you like some magazines?
Barbara No, please—I don't feel like reading.
Helen Are you sure?
Barbara (*nodding*) I think I'd rather just go to sleep.
Helen Okay, you know best.

Helen goes to the front door; Barbara follows

Now look—if there's anything I can do—and I mean anything ...
Barbara That's very kind of you, Helen.
Helen Well, for God's sake—what are friends for? (*She smiles at Barbara*) You take care of yourself.
Barbara You too.
Helen Go right upstairs and have a good long rest.
Barbara Yes, I will.
Helen Good girl. See you tomorrow. *Ciao.*

Helen opens the front door and goes out

Barbara closes the front door. She shuts her eyes and leans back against the wall. Suddenly, she feels the bile rising in her throat; she runs to the kitchen and vomits into the sink

Thelma walks down the stairs; she pauses halfway

Thelma Mrs Jackson ...?

No response

Are you all right, Mrs Jackson?
Barbara Leave me alone—just leave me alone!

The Lights fade

Thelma and Barbara exit. Bob and Stewart enter the hall

The Lights come up. Evening. Bob and Stewart go into the sitting-room. Stewart removes his coat

Stewart I hope you don't think I've been neglecting you, Mr Jackson.
Bob No no.
Stewart I've been meaning to come round, but the days just flash by, don't

they? (*He turns to face Bob*) I gather from my girls that your wife is becoming increasingly unhappy with the, um ... (*Pause*) Is she?

Bob Well, yes.

Stewart You should have told me. (*Pause*) There's not much I can do.

Bob No.

Stewart You do understand that, don't you? Well, of course you do, I know you do. You're a reasonable man, after all.

Pause

Bob Can I get you a drink, sir?

Stewart Thank you very much. Whisky and water, if that's all right.

Bob goes to fetch a drink for Stewart and himself. Stewart glances at his wristwatch

What time does she get back from her art club?

Bob Any minute now.

Stewart Oh good. (*He takes his cigarette pack from his jacket pocket*) May I?

Bob Please.

Stewart Would it help, do you think, if I tried to clarify the situation a little?

Bob How do you mean?

Stewart Perhaps she feels she's being kept in the dark. Does she? Is that the problem, do you think?

Bob Something like that, yes.

Stewart Well, in that case, it's a problem easily solved. (*He smiles; pause*) By the way, I meant to ask: somebody was saying that you and the Krogers have got the same sort of car—is that right?

Bob Yes.

Stewart You've both got black Ford Consuls?

Bob Yes.

Stewart How extraordinary.

No response

Or perhaps it isn't. What do you think?

Bob There are plenty of Consuls about—specially round here.

Stewart Yes, true. (*Brief pause*) Nevertheless—to find two black Ford Consuls owned by such close neighbours—I must say that strikes me as being rather ... well, rather surprising.

No response

How did it happen? Whose car came first?

Bob Ours. Helen said how nice it was, how smart, and so on—and then Peter told me they were going to get one exactly the same.

Stewart Uh-huh. (*Brief pause*) Is he a car person? Is he interested in cars?

Bob No, not particularly.

Stewart He just took a fancy to yours ...

Bob Well, yes.

Stewart (*smiling*) Well, why not? It's a very nice car. What are his interests?
Does he have any hobbies?

Bob Nothing special. I don't think, um . . . (*Pause*) Books, of course. Apart
from that . . . nothing much. (*Pause*) He likes music. He listen to music a
lot.

Stewart On the radio?

Bob And records. He's got quite a collection.

Stewart Don't tell me he's one of these hi-fi fanatics.

Bob Well, a bit, I suppose—stereo sound, FM radio, headphones, you
know, rumble filters. All that sort of stuff.

Stewart Headphones . . .?

Bob He likes classical music and she doesn't. She can't stand it. So he listens
to his records through the headphones.

Stewart Well, that's one way of avoiding domestic strife, I suppose. What
about Mrs Kroger? Does she have a hobby?

Bob No, not really. She's too much of a Dizzy Lizzy to do anything
properly. Poor old Helen. She makes us laugh.

Stewart How often do you go to the Krogers' house?

Bob Hardly ever. Barbara pops in for a cup of tea most weeks, but as far as
I'm concerned—well, four or five times a year—birthdays, Christmas,
that sort of thing, you know.

Stewart nods, pause

Peter works at home—I think we told you. That makes it a bit difficult.
We're always afraid of disturbing him.

Stewart Yes, quite. Apart from you, does Mrs Kroger have any particular
friends?

Bob She's friendly with everyone. She's a very friendly woman.

Stewart In what way?

Bob (*not understanding the question*) What?

Stewart How does this friendliness manifest itself?

Bob (*irritated*) She's just an ordinary friendly woman. She pops in for a
chat, she worries if anything's wrong, she takes an interest in people,
that's all.

Stewart Takes an interest . . .?

Bob Well, you know.

Stewart Perhaps you could give me an example.

Bob (*angrily*) I don't often see her, Mr Stewart, I'm at work when she comes
round; Barbara's the one she talks to, not me. I don't know what she does
or what she says. Anyway, there's nothing sinister about being friendly, is
there?

Stewart Nothing sinister, no. It just adds to the pattern.

Bob Pattern?

Stewart Well, if the Krogers are mixed up in this business—and I say if—if
they are, then it would be essential for them to know what's going on.
Any change of routine, any change of neighbour . . . it could be dangerous
for them.

Bob You can make anything look suspicious if you try hard enough.

Stewart True.

Bob I mean, all that stuff about the cars. Why shouldn't they buy a car like ours if they want to?

Stewart No reason at all—on the other hand, it could be construed as an extremely clever thing to do.

Bob Clever, why?

Stewart Because it would certainly confuse anyone who might be watching them; I mean, if one of my chaps saw a black Ford Consul parked in Cranley Drive he couldn't be sure, at a glance, whether the Krogers were at home or whether you were. Might be useful, that.

Bob stares at Stewart; he says nothing

It's not terribly important, I agree—it's just one of those little details that tend to arouse interest. And it's only when you start adding all these things together that a significant pattern begins to emerge.

Barbara enters; she is wearing her tweed coat and carrying a shopping bag filled with oil-paints and brushes

Barbara (*calling*) It's only me.

Bob (*calling*) We're in here.

Barbara goes to the sitting-room. She stares at Stewart

Barbara Mr Stewart.

Stewart Do forgive me for dropping in like this. I just wanted to make sure that everything is all right. (*Brief pause*) Is everything all right?

Barbara puts down her shopping bag and unbuttons her coat. Pause

Barbara I thought the girls would be going last weekend.

Stewart Well—no, I'm terribly sorry.

Bob Mr Stewart says he'll explain.

Barbara First it was two days, then a week, then two weeks . . . how much longer?

Stewart responds with a friendly smile

Stewart Let me put you in the picture, shall I? Let me tell you something about the background to this case. It won't solve your problems, I know, but it may help you to live with them for just a little longer.

Brief pause. Barbara turns to Bob

Barbara Have you offered Mr Stewart a cup of tea?

Bob Yes, I——

Stewart Thank you, Mrs Jackson. Your husband has been most hospitable.

Barbara goes to the door

Barbara I'll just take my coat off.

Barbara goes to the hall and hangs her coat on a peg. Stewart turns to Bob

Stewart Julie's gone to the cinema, I believe?

Bob Yes.

Stewart Yes, I thought it would be a good idea to come when she was out. Fewer complications. (*A smile*) And the fewer of them the better, eh? (*Pause*) What has she gone to see?

Bob Um ... I'm not sure.

Barbara returns

(*To Barbara*) What's Julie gone to see?

Barbara *The Millionairess.*

Stewart Oh, that's frightfully good. We enjoyed it enormously. Peter Sellers is marvellous. First-class.

Barbara turns abruptly to Stewart

Barbara Look, since you're here, there's something I must tell you.

Stewart (*friendly*) What's that?

Barbara I don't know how much longer I can go on like this.

Brief pause

Stewart Yes. Yes, I'm sorry.

Barbara Apart from anything else, I'm worried about Julie—she's got so much work to do for her exams, and all this is very unsettling for her.

Stewart Yes, of course.

Barbara I know it's important, what you're doing here, but we have got our own lives to lead, after all. You must have known it would be more than a couple of days. You should have told us.

Stewart It's always difficult to know how long these jobs will take.

Barbara It's getting worse—much worse.

Stewart Yes, I'm sure.

Barbara Seeing Helen and Peter.

Stewart Yes.

Barbara Every time I see her, every time she comes round ... it makes me feel quite ill. (*Brief pause*) I can't sleep.

Stewart Well, if it's any comfort to you, we still don't know how they fit into this, uh ... into this particular puzzle. Obviously they must fit in somehow. I mean, as friends of Lonsdale's they must have a place somewhere. But how or where or why, we don't yet know. Maybe they met him in Canada—and since he's travelling on a Canadian passport, that's a distinct possibility. But, at the moment, all we can do is speculate. (*Brief pause*) Sorry I can't be more ... reassuring.

Bob What about Lonsdale? Do you know anything more about him?

Stewart Anything more ...?

Bob You said he might be a spy of some sort. Is he? You weren't quite sure.

Stewart Ah yes. (*He glances at Bob, surprised, perhaps, to realize how little information has been imparted*) Well—well ... Since the last war, submarines have become an increasingly important element in defence strategy—both for us and NATO and—most especially—the Russians. They have a vast fleet of submarines—at least seven hundred, probably more. But the effective value of this fleet has been drastically reduced by the various techniques of underwater detection that have been developed by our NATO chaps—ASDICs, sonar buoys, and so on. Needless to say, Moscow is most anxious to learn the secrets of these devices. And so spies were sent here to find out all they could. The man in charge of this operation is the man who visits your friends every weekend, the man calling himself Gordon Lonsdale.

Bob Good God.

Stewart Oh yes, he's an important chap, make no mistake about that—almost certainly a high-ranking officer in the KGB: Russian Intelligence. And so far, he's been remarkably successful. But the trouble with spying is that you can't always rely on fellow professionals: You often need the help of amateurs. Traitors. And such creatures can be notoriously unstable. Lonsdale needed inside help; and eventually he found a suitable collaborator, an Englishman called Harry. We became interested in Harry about a year ago. He's a naval man, works at the Underwater Weapons Establishment. Fiftyish, not much of a career, divorced. A bit of a boozer. In fact, he's been boozing rather a lot recently—spending a lot of money in local pubs, far more than he can reasonably afford. And always with the same girlfriend; so we decided to keep an eye on her and we discovered that she works in the same establishment—in the records section where all the secret material on underwater weapons is filed. They're always together—every evening: eating, drinking in plush restaurants. And there's never any shortage of cash. Where do they get it? (*Brief pause*) They come to London about once a month. They meet Lonsdale; they give him the secrets so earnestly desired by the Russians; and he gives them the cash.

Pause. Barbara and Bob stare at each other, almost unable to believe their ears

Barbara But ... but if you think that ... why haven't you arrested them?

Stewart (*smiling*) Yes, that's what the Admiralty wants to know. We've had several sharp memos about it. But the point is, there are bound to be others involved—not just Harry and his girlfriend—not just Lonsdale—there are bound to be others, and we want to catch the whole lot. That's why we've got to keep watching Lonsdale for just a few more days. The kettle's already bubbling; we must wait for it to boil.

Pause

Barbara Do you mean watching Lonsdale, or do you mean watching Helen and Peter?

Stewart I mean, watching everyone who's been in regular contact with him. Everyone. And anyone.

Pause

Bob Are you quite sure there isn't any danger?

Stewart To you? Absolutely none.

Bob What about Barbara and Julie? They're on their own here most of the time—and I keep thinking—if this man Lonsdale gets frightened or suspicious—what then?

Stewart There'll be no violence, I can assure you of that. The KGB don't
employ hooligans for this sort of operation.

Barbara How can you be sure?

Stewart Because I am.

Barbara How can you be?

Stewart Because it's my job to be—and I'm very good at my job.

Bob It's all very well for you, you're used to this sort of thing. I mean, all
this talk of the Russians and the KGB . . .

Stewart Yes, it must seem very alarming.

Bob Well, it is alarming.

Stewart Not as far as you and I are concerned.

Barbara I wish I could believe that.

Stewart There's absolutely no need to worry, I know what I'm talking
about. I have spent most of my adult life studying the supposedly secret
workings of Russian Intelligence. It's a fascinating task—rather like bird-
watching. And just as a bird-watcher gets to know the most intimate
habits of his favourite species, so I know how these fellows operate. I
know their methods. And it's not just guesswork. You'd be amazed what
you can find out when you try hard enough. For example . . . I know more
about the KGB Chairman than I do about my next-door neighbour. His
name's Shelepin—(*a small smile*)—the KGB chap, not my next-door
neighbour, Aleksandr Nikolaevich Shelepin. He's got a flat in the
Kutuzovsky Prospekt—very nice, too, palatial by Soviet standards; and
it's furnished with all those little luxuries that only the chosen members of
the Party elite are able to enjoy: TV, radiogram, piano, bottles of real
scotch in the sideboard. He always has an early breakfast; eggs, ham,
black Russian bread, tea, a nip of brandy, and then, at eight-fifteen, a
chauffeur-driven car takes him to Moscow Centre, the KGB headquarters
in Dzerzhinsky Square. It's quite a pleasant building: grey stone, looks
more Flemish than Russian; it used to belong to an insurance company
before the Revolution. A harmless-looking place. You wouldn't give it a
second glance. But there's a courtyard tucked away behind and in that
courtyard is the Lubyanka Prison, where hundreds of people have died.
Thousands. (*Pause*) Shelepin's office is on the third floor. It's got a high
ceiling, polished parquet, a couple of old-fashioned sofas, wood-panelled
walls. There are six telephones on his desk, one of which is a direct line to
the Kremlin. He often works long hours, so there's a bedroom next door
in case he's kept late by some particularly intransigent problem. (*Brief
pause*) Sometimes he strolls across the Persian carpet and looks down at
the people hurry along the Marx Prospekt. He controls those people and
they know it. You could, I suppose, say much the same about any senior
civil servant looking down at the rush-hour crowds in Whitehall. But
there's one big difference: Shelepin's control is absolute. (*Pause*) He's
youngish, too—not yet forty-three. He likes sport, particularly football,
and he enjoys going to the theatre. What's more he's got a weakness for
ice-cream, which is not surprising because Russian ice-cream is the best in
the world. "*Morozhennoe pazhahlsta*" is a phrase that every tourist should
memorize; it means "Ice-cream, please." Anyone who goes to Russia

should make a point of trying the ice-cream. (*He smiles*) And all I know about my next-door neighbour is that his name is Warrender and that he subscribes to the *National Geographic* magazine. (*Pause*) So the answer to your question is no, there's no danger, absolutely not. The merest hint of any strong-arm behaviour would cause the most almighty diplomatic rumpus—and that's the one thing the Soviets want to avoid at all costs. So there's nothing to worry about. I guarantee it. (*Turning to Barbara*) Does that put your mind at rest, Mrs Jackson? There's nothing to worry about.

Pause. Bob and Stewart look at Barbara, waiting for her response. She rises to her feet

Barbara So the girls will be here for some time, then?
Stewart Well, I hope not—for all our sakes. A few days, perhaps. That's the plan.
Barbara Yes, I see. (*She manages the ghost of a smile*) Well, if you'll excuse me, I've got some jobs to do. (*She goes to the door*) Is that all right? Do you mind if I go?
Stewart No no, of course not. Thank you for being so patient.
Barbara I don't have much choice, do I?

Barbara goes to the kitchen, where she stands staring out of the window. Stewart turns to Bob and smiles

Stewart I'm not quite sure what I expected her to say, but I certainly expected more than that.
Bob She never says much when she's upset.
Stewart No, well ... some people don't. (*Pause*) It must be the most frightful strain. Appalling.
Bob Yes.
Stewart If you think it's getting too much for her, you will let me know, won't you? Just telephone Superintendent Smith; I'll pop around any time.
Bob Right.
Stewart Good. Well—I'd better be going. (*He picks up his overcoat*) Don't forget—day or night—don't hesitate to ring. (*Putting on his overcoat*) On the other hand, of course, some women can be remarkably tough. I've noticed it time and time again. Tough and resilient. Much more so than many men. Oh yes.

Bob nods, but says nothing. Stewart goes to the kitchen. Bob follows

Good-night, Mrs Jackson.
Barbara Good-night.
Stewart How are my young ladies behaving themselves? No problems in that department, I trust?
Barbara Oh no, they're very quiet and considerate.
Stewart Good. I'm glad to hear it. (*He turns to Bob and shakes him by the hand*) I'm most grateful, Mr Jackson. Thank you for being so cooperative. Good-night.

Bob Good-night, Mr Stewart.

Bob opens the back door

   Stewart exits

Bob closes the door. He looks at Barbara. Aware of his gaze, she glances at him

Barbara Tea or cocoa? Which would you like? Tea or cocoa?

Bob goes to her

Bob Look, I know how you feel. But it was good of him to come round and explain all those things. I mean, he didn't have to.

Barbara busies herself at the sink

Barbara I've made up my mind what I'm going to do: I'm not going to think about it. We've got to lead a normal life—for Julie's sake, if not our own. Let them do what they like. I'm not going to think about it. (*She fills the electric kettle with water*) Tea or cocoa?
Bob Tea, I think.
Barbara Right. Go and sit down, I'll bring it in.

The Lights fade

   Bob exits

Barbara walks downstage and addresses the audience

Barbara Bob's mother was such a frail little thing. I never knew his father; he died long before we met. He was a clerk with an insurance company. She lived alone, Bob's mother, she lived alone in a small draughty house in Canterbury. She used to visit us twice a year, but she always went home after a week. "I don't want to be any trouble," she'd say. It was the most important thing in all her life—not being any trouble. When her roof leaked, she refused to tell the landlord. "He's been very good to me," she said. "I don't want to make a fuss." When she was ill and dying, she wouldn't call the doctor after six o'clock in the evening. She'd lay alone in that miserable house, more worried about making a fuss than anything else. Her life was governed by fear, bless her heart. She was afraid of post office clerks, bus conductors, anyone in uniform. And, like a child, she thought if she kept very still and didn't say anything, nobody would take any notice of her. And she was right—they didn't.

The Lights come up. Late afternoon

Barbara goes to the sitting-room. She fetches a cardboard box, some tissue paper and the now-completed dress for Helen. She starts to fold the dress

Thelma walks down the stairs: she is wearing a raincoat and headscarf. She knocks on the sitting-room door and enters

   Don't tell me it's half-past.
Thelma Mr Stewart said I could leave early.

Glancing up, Barbara sees that Thelma is not wearing her usual motorcycling gear

Barbara No bike today?
Thelma Trouble with the clutch. (*She looks at the dress*) Who's that for?
Barbara (*somewhat embarrassed*) Actually—Helen. I promised it to her ages ago.
Thelma It's lovely. Really professional.
Barbara Well, hardly.
Thelma It is—really. You are lucky—having a talent like that.
Barbara I wouldn't call it much of a talent, Thelma.
Thelma Well, I think it is. I was hopeless at needlework when I was at school. Hopeless at needlework, dreadful at art. Everything I did looked the same: trees, people, buildings—you couldn't tell one from the other. Cats, flowers, elephants—they all looked the same.

Barbara smiles: Thelma buttons her raincoat

I wish I had a hobby like you, I wish there was something I could do really well.
Barbara Oh, I'm sure there is.
Thelma (*cheerfully*) No, there's not. There never has been. I can do lots of things sort of half well—but nothing really tip-top. I don't stick at things long enough, that's my trouble. It's what Dad calls my grasshopper mind. (*She grins*) Well, I'll see you tomorrow. Usual time.
Barbara Yes, right.
Thelma I'm coming in instead of Pat. She's got a filthy cold.
Barbara Right.

Thelma goes to the door; Barbara plucks up courage to summon her back

Thelma . . .

Thelma pauses by the door

Is there any news?
Thelma News . . .?
Barbara Yes, news. Nobody tells us anything.
Thelma Well, no. Not as far as I know.

Barbara looks directly at Thelma

Barbara Mr Stewart came to see us.
Thelma Yes. Yes, I know that.
Barbara He told us about Harry and his girlfriend. And the Russians, what they're trying to do, what they're trying to find out.
Thelma Yes.
Barbara Did you know he was coming?
Thelma Well, yes.
Barbara You never said anything about it.

No response

Did he?

No response

He didn't even mention Helen and Peter. I mean he didn't tell us whether they're—you know—actually ... (*The sentence drifts away into silence*)

Thelma says nothing

Well, of course they must be involved. It's obvious. Any fool can see that. (*Looking at Thelma*) Why didn't he tell us?

Thelma Well, I can't ...

Pause

Barbara What?
Thelma You know I can't tell you anything.
Barbara Why not?
Thelma You know I can't.
Barbara (*angry*) So you think it's all right, do you, just to let things go on like this.
Thelma Well, no, I mean——
Barbara (*overlapping*) You think that's all right, do you? Is that what you think?
Thelma (*firmly*) If I could do anything, I would—but I can't.

Silence. Barbara sighs. Her head bows forward. She sits motionless

Barbara To tell you the truth, Thelma, I don't really care. I don't care what they've done. Helen and Peter. It doesn't make any difference. Not now. (*Pause; she raises her head and looks at Thelma*) Isn't that strange? I don't really care. I cared at first, of course. When I first thought, when I first realized ... all the deceit and lies and ... I was so angry, I was so hurt—I was so *hurt*, Thelma ... and I wanted—well, I don't know what I wanted. I wanted them to be punished, I suppose; I wanted them to be taken away and punished. But those feelings don't last very long, do they? And I keep thinking how kind she's been—and she has been very kind. She's been very kind to Julie. (*Pause*) I don't care what she's done, she's still my friend. (*Pause; she sits motionless*) I'll tell you what chokes me, Thelma: it's that Mr Stewart not telling us anything, not telling us about Helen and Peter, treating us like a couple of kids who can't be trusted. How dare he! (*Pause*) Can you imagine what it's been like? Can you?

No response

Last Friday, when I went shopping, I looked at the women all round me. And I thought, "I'm not like them. I'm not like the others. I may look like them, but I'm not." (*Pause*) It hurts telling all these lies. It really hurts. It's like a dead weight on my stomach. It's like grief. You can't forget it. (*Pause*) And he won't tell us. Why not? Does he think we can't be trusted. Does he think we're too stupid to understand? Or perhaps he thinks it doesn't matter. (*A shaft of bitterness*) Well, that's it, of course—why should he bother about us? We're the sort of people who stand in queues and don't answer back. Why should he bother? We'll just do as we're told and not ask any questions. (*Pause—and then with a sudden passion*) Well, I hate him! *I hate him!* I want to smack his smiling face and say, "How dare you! How dare you treat us like that! Who the hell do you think you are!" (*Pause; her passion subsides*) I won't though, will I? Of course I won't. I can say all these things to you because you're just Thelma who likes Richard Burton and sausages for lunch. But I can't tell him and he knows it. That's how it works, of course. That's how he gets his own way.

Pause. Silence

Thelma Look, I'm sorry.

Barbara raises her head and looks at Thelma

Barbara I bet he knew when he first came here, didn't he?
Thelma Knew what?
Barbara About Helen and Peter.
Thelma I don't know.
Barbara I thought it seemed incredible at the time; seeing Lonsdale that first Sunday.
Thelma It could have been a coincidence.
Barbara Could it?
Thelma Well, I don't know. Mr Stewart doesn't tell me anything, either. I just do what I'm told.
Barbara I suppose that's what he'd say, isn't it?
Thelma He might.

Pause

Barbara If only it hadn't been us. If only it hadn't been Helen and Peter. I lie awake every night thinking, "Why them . . . why us?" (*Pause*) This time last year, everything was so perfect.

Pause. Thelma takes Barbara by the hand

Thelma I'll tell you what I think: it's a waste of time looking for reasons. That's what I think. Good things happen, bad things happen. One day you win the pools, the next you fall down stairs. Nobody's to blame. It's nobody's fault. These things just happen. Start looking for reasons and you'll go barmy. (*She grins*) Honest. Trust me. Thelma knows. (*She squeezes Barbara's hand*) Can I get you something? How about a nice cup of tea?

Barbara smiles

Barbara You're just like my husband. He thinks a cup of tea will cure anything.

Thelma smiles. Barbara rises to her feet

   Off you go. The buses will be packed.
Thelma Are you sure you're all right?

Barbara nods

I'll see you tomorrow, then.

Barbara nods

I'm sorry.
Barbara It's not your fault.
Thelma It's nobody's fault. You just remember that. (*She goes to the sitting-room door*)

The front door opens and Julie enters, returning from school

Julie Hello, Thelma, how are you?
Thelma Fine, thanks—how are you?
Julie Fine—where's Mum?

Barbara emerges from the sitting-room

Barbara Here I am. (*She kisses Julie*) Had a good day?
Julie Pretty gruesome.

Thelma goes towards the kitchen

Thelma Bye, then, see you tomorrow.
Barbara Bye, Thelma. I hope you get your bike back soon.
Thelma Yes, so do I. (*To Julie, as she opens the kitchen door*) I'll have to ask your boyfriend to give me a lift. That's a smashing bike he's got. What is it, a Triumph?

Julie's mouth falls open in dismay. Barbara stares at her, appalled

Barbara Julie . . .!
Julie He was only giving me a ride home.
Barbara How many times have we told you?
Julie Yes, I know——
Barbara (*overlapping*) How many times?
Julie (*overlapping*) Yes, I'm sorry——
Barbara (*overlapping*) And you promised. You gave your word!
Julie I'm sorry, Mum. I'm sorry!
Barbara So that's the sort of daughter I've got—somebody who goes behind my back——
Julie (*overlapping*) I'm sorry!
Barbara (*overlapping*) —somebody who lies and cheats!
Julie I'm sorry, I'm sorry!
Barbara I'll never be able to trust you ever again—never again—never!

Julie bursts into tears and runs upstairs

Julie I'm sorry, I'm sorry, I'm sorry, I'm sorry!

Julie exits

A door slams. Silence. Barbara stands, trembling and breathless, momentarily exhausted by her outburst. Thelma remains standing by the kitchen door. Barbara sobs. The Lights fade

Barbara and Thelma exit. Peter enters and addresses the audience

During the following, Barbara, Bob, Julie and Helen enter the sitting-room

Peter In the winter of nineteen thirty-two, when the Depression was at its worst, a friend took me to a meeting—an informal and private meeting—in New York City. On our way there, we walked along Riverside Drive. Literally hundreds of unemployed and hungry men were camping there in tiny shacks and shanties. I saw in their faces a degree of hopelessness and despair I had never seen before. (*Brief pause*) I remembered those brave words about "life, liberty, and the pursuit of happiness". And I felt a sudden surge of anger that such noble ideals should have been betrayed—forgotten. Why did it happen—how? (*Brief pause*) When I got to the meeting, I found a small group of maybe seven or eight men and women, mostly young, mostly about my age. It was cold that night, and there was no heat in the apartment; we stood around wearing overcoats. An older man read to us from the works of Marx and Lenin. He had a soft voice; gentle; I've never forgotten it. He said, "The ruin of capitalism is imminent. Every attempt to establish a truly human society upon the old capitalist foundations is foredoomed to absolute failure. We are thus confronted by two alternatives, and two only. There must be either complete disintegration, further brutalization and disorder; absolute chaos, or else Communism." (*Brief pause*) That evening, my whole life changed.

The Lights came up. Evening

A Christmas tree, decorated with coloured lights, stands in the sitting-room. Barbara, Bob, Julie and Helen are grouped around the tree singing a carol. Peter joins them

All   With the Angelic host proclaim,
                                 "Christ is born in Bethlehem."
                                 Hark! the herald-angels sing
                                 Glory to the new-born King!

Julie and Helen cheer. Helen is slightly drunk

Helen Hey—wasn't that something?
Julie Wonderful!
Helen Terrific! Come on, let's have a drink . . . (*taking a bottle of sherry from the coffee-table*) . . . one more little drink . . .
Peter (*stepping forward anxiously*) I think it's time to go home.
Helen Time to go home? Whaddya mean—time to go home? What are you talking about? I don't want to go home—I'm having fun! (*To Julie*) How about a drink for you, honey-chile?
Julie (*glancing at Bob, seeking his permission*) Well, I . . .
Bob There's some lemonade in the kitchen.
Helen Come on, Bob, a glass of sherry won't do her any harm. Let the girl live a little. Jeeze—when I was her age I was drinking bourbon like it was mother's milk! (*She laughs raucously*)

Peter Helen, please ...

Helen Get off my back, will you? Stop nagging! Don't be such a goddam spoil-sport.

Peter (*sharper*) Helen.

Helen swings round to face him; her initial reaction seems to be one of anger; brief pause; her mood changes, and she becomes immediately contrite

Helen Okay. Okay. Sorry. (*She grins*) Loudmouth Helen does it again. "You never know when to stop. You always go too far." Jesus, how many times have I heard that! (*Smiling at Peter*) Okay—just one more little drink, then home. Okay?

Peter It's getting late.

Helen So what? It's Christmastime—I'm with my friends—and I'm happy. Come on; relax. (*Turning to Julie*) Hey—do you know what this reminds me of? Christmas at Aunt Sophie's. We always went to Aunt Sophie's when I was a kid—every Christmas. She had the most beautiful little house. Beautiful. And she loved brass—there was brass everywhere: kettles, spark guard, candlesticks, a great brass pot filled with indoor plants. A log fire and gleaming brass. And she'd do everything as it was when she was a kid. We always had a roast goose and chocolate honey-cake. And there she'd sit, after dinner, my old Aunt Sophie, licking her fingers to pick up the crumbs of chocolate honey-cake—and all of a sudden she'd burst out crying. "What's the matter?" we'd say. "Why are you crying, Aunt Sophie?" And she'd dry her eyes and blow her nose and lick her chocolatey fingers. "Nothing's the matter," she'd say. "I'm crying because everything's just poifeck." (*She smiles*) Well, I reckon that's how I feel right now.

Moved by this story, Julie goes to Helen and embraces her. Helen kisses Julie on the forehead. The telephone rings

Julie That'll be Maureen.

Julie goes to the hall. Helen looks at Barbara, Bob, and Peter—three unsmiling faces

Helen Oh, come on, you guys. It's party-time, remember? Jesus, I've had more laughs at a funeral. Come on—let's goose it up a little!

Julie (*calling from the hall*) It's for you, Dad. It's Mr Stewart.

Bob glances sharply at Barbara, and hurries to the phone

Bob Right.

Barbara unable to move or speak, just watches him go. Julie returns to the sitting-room

Helen Stewart ... Stewart ... I've heard that name before ... Stewart Granger ... James Stewart ... Hey, did you see James Stewart in *Vertigo*? He was terrific—*terrific*!

Nobody responds. Helen reaches for another drink

I think I'll have another drink. Don't look at me like that, Peter—it's just one for the road—one more for the road, okay?

Bob comes back into the sitting-room. Barbara scarcely dares speak to him. She rises to her feet

Bob Merry Christmas. That's all. He just said, "Merry Christmas". A bit late in the day. Still—nice of him.

Helen begins to sing boisterously "We wish you a Merry Christmas". Julie, Peter, and Bob join in. Eventually even Barbara begins to sing with them. The Lights fade

Barbara, Bob, Peter, and Julie exit; the Christmas tree is removed

Helen moves downstage and addresses the audience

Helen In nineteen fifty we had an apartment on East Seventy-First Street—nothing fancy, but I loved it. I've never been much of a home-maker—anyone will tell you that—but that place was special, it was the kind of place I always wanted. The sun streamed in through the kitchen window. It was all yellow and bright and cheery and warm. I even made curtains for that window. One evening, Peter came home early. "We've got to leave," he said. "The Rosenbergs have been arrested. We've got to leave." I looked at Peter. His mouth had gone dry; he moistened his lips with his tongue. "When?" I asked. "Tonight," he said. "We've got to get the hell out of here as fast as we can." And that's what we did. We left our clothes in the closet, books on the shelves, food in the refrigerator. We could've stayed, I suppose, and taken our chances—but we didn't. And from then on, there was no turning back.

The Lights fade

Helen exits. Barbara, Bob and Stewart enter the kitchen

The Lights come up. Day

Barbara and Bob are in the kitchen; they stand facing Stewart, who has just entered

Stewart I'm sorry to disturb your Saturday, but I thought you'd be glad to know that it'll soon be over.
Barbara Over . . .?
Stewart As far as you're concerned, anyway.
Barbara The girls will be going.
Stewart They will indeed.
Bob When?
Stewart As from today.

Barbara and Bob stare at each other, amazed

Bob What do you mean?
Barbara What's happened? I mean—why today? Has anything happened?

Stewart Not yet. But with any luck ... (*He allows the sentence to drift away into an infuriatingly ambiguous silence*)
Barbara (*sharply*) What? With any luck, what?

Stewart responds to the anger in her voice; his reply is unusually direct and unveiled

Stewart Harry—the man I told you about—he's on his way to London with his girlfriend. We believe that they will have another meeting with Lonsdale. And if they do, we shall arrest them.

A moment of silence

Bob What about Helen and Peter?
Stewart (*evenly*) Yes, we'll pick them up this afternoon. If everything goes according to plan.
Barbara This afternoon ... (*She sits suddenly, heavily*)
Bob What have they done?
Stewart They're Lonsdale's transmitting station. He brings them information which they dispatch to KGB headquaters, either hidden in the books that Peter Kroger posts to fictitious clients in various parts of Europe, or presumably by radio. I'm sorry to tell you so bluntly, but there's no doubt about it: your friends are both Communist agents with many years' experience behind them. And their name's not Kroger by the way, and they're American—not Canadian. I thought it better that you hear it from me rather than read about it in the newspapers.

Barbara and Bob remain motionless, stunned

Barbara When I think of the hours she's spent in this house ... in this room ... (*She lapses into silence for a moment; she looks up at Stewart*) Was it *all* a lie—I mean everything she's ever told us? (*Almost imploringly*) Was it?
Stewart Well, not everything, I suppose.
Barbara I mean, all those stories about her life on the farm—wasn't that the truth?
Stewart Apparently not. Her parents emigrated from Poland. They lived in a place called Utica in New York State. Her father was fairly well-off; he made his money during Prohibition. He was a bootlegger. (*Brief pause*) Peter Kroger was a schoolteacher. He became a Communist in the thirties and fought in the Spanish Civil War.

Pause

Barbara How could she do it? How *could* she? I've never had many friends, not close friends, not what you'd call close ... never. (*Brief pause; she struggles to prevent herself from weeping*) But I trusted Helen. I thought she was brash and noisy and sometimes a bit silly ... but I trusted her. I loved her.
Stewart (*sympathetically*) Well, I'm quite sure that her affection for you is perfectly genuine. There's no reason to doubt that.
Barbara (*angrily*) No reason ...? What do you mean, no reason? There's every reason to doubt everything she's ever said or done!

Stewart Yes, well, you're bound to feel like that. And there's nothing anyone can do to soften the blow. I only wish there were.

A moment of silence

Barbara I tell you what I wish, Mr Stewart. I wish you had never come here.

Bob, startled by these words, swings round towards Barbara

Stewart (*gently*) Yes, I'm sure ...

Barbara I wish you'd never set foot inside this house!

Bob Don't let's start blaming Mr Stewart—it's not his fault.

Barbara (*to Stewart, ignoring Bob*) Helen may have lied to us—but you've gone one better. You made us do the lying; we've even lied to our own daughter.

Bob We haven't *lied* to her.

Barbara We haven't told her the truth, have we? What's she going to do when she finds out?

Bob She'll understand.

Barbara Will she?

Bob Of course she will.

Stewart I'm sure she'll realize you were only trying to protect her.

Barbara Oh, do stop making excuses! Helen's lying and we're lying—we're all playing the same rotten game.

Stewart Well, hardly.

Barbara Of course we are. What's the difference between one lie and another? (*Her anger rising*) When I hear you making excuses for what we've done, I feel sick with fear—physically sick! People like you can find excuses for anything.

Bob steps forward, anxious to make peace

Bob Look, there's no sense in upsetting yourself like this.

Barbara I'm not upsetting myself! I'm trying to explain how I feel—I'm trying to face up to the fact that I have betrayed Helen as much as she has betrayed me.

Stewart That's just not so.

Barbara Isn't it?

Bob Of course not.

Silence

Sally emerges from upstairs, wearing outdoor clothes and carrying an unplugged telephone. She walks downstairs and taps on the kitchen door, opening it a fraction

Sally Excuse me, sir, I'm going now.

Stewart Yes, all right.

Sally exits

Stewart turns to Bob

I think I'd better come back tomorrow, don't you? When everything's

over and done with. (*He turns to Barbara*) Try not to judge yourself too harshly, Mrs Jackson. It won't do anybody any good—least of all yourself.
Barbara (*quietly*) What'll happen to them?
Stewart The Krogers? They'll be sent for trial, I suppose. And then imprisoned.

Barbara's head bows forward

Barbara But they love each other. They're happy together and now they'll be separated. Maybe forever.

Stewart gazes at Barbara; he sighs

Stewart I'm sorry I've caused you so much pain. I only wish there was something I could do. (*A small smile*) I keep saying the same old thing, don't I? But there's nothing else I can say; nothing I can do; nothing any of us can do.
Barbara You could have told us the truth. You knew all this ages ago. Why didn't you tell us?

Stewart hesitates briefly before he replies

Stewart I had to be careful. You might have warned the Krogers.
Barbara What makes you think I won't now?
Stewart (*attempting a confident smile*) Well.
Barbara If I was brave enough, I would. I would. Really, I would. (*Her eyes fill with tears*) If I was brave enough, I'd go across the road—I'd bang on the door, and I'd say to them, "Get out—get out before they catch you—please, please, get out—please ...!"

She runs to the sitting-room; Stewart and Bob follow. The front doorbell rings. Barbara looks out of the window

Barbara It's Helen!

They all converse in hushed, urgent whispers

Bob It can't be!
Barbara Well, it is.

The doorbell rings again

Stewart (*to Bob*) Answer the door. Answer the door, Mr Jackson.

Barbara flees to the kitchen. Bob goes to the hall. Stewart follows Barbara. Bob opens the front door

Helen enters

Helen Hi, Bob—how's life?
Bob Oh well, you know. Not so bad.
Helen Is Barbara home?
Bob Well, yes—but she's feeling a bit off-colour.
Helen Off-colour ...?
Bob Tired, you know.

Helen goes to the sitting-room; Bob follows. Barbara struggles to recover her composure; she goes to the sitting-room

Helen Why didn't you call me? I'd have come over and cooked lunch.
Bob She's not ill—just tired.

Barbara enters the sitting-room

Helen Barbara, honey—what is it? What's the matter?
Barbara It's nothing—really.
Bob She's got a rotten headache.
Helen Again? You ought to see a doctor, honey.
Barbara Yes, well . . .
Helen You make her go, Bob—she won't go unless you make her.
Bob Yes, I will.

Helen goes to Barbara

Helen Gee, you're looking real pale. Are you sure it's just a headache?
Barbara Quite sure.
Bob She's just tired.
Helen There's a lot of flu about. Maybe it's flu.
Barbara It's just another silly headache.

Satisfied that the Jacksons will not reveal any secrets. Stewart exits through the kitchen door

Helen Headaches aren't silly. (*Glancing at Barbara*) Are you sure there's nothing wrong?
Barbara (*a little too sharply*) Wrong?
Bob (*hastily*) No no, she's all right.
Helen It's not like you, getting all these headaches. You've had three in a month.
Barbara I suppose I'm worried, that's all.
Helen What about?
Barbara Oh—this and that . . . things, you know.
Helen What things?
Barbara Well, nothing special, nothing in particular, nothing serious.

Helen sits beside Barbara

Helen Now, come on—don't be shy. You just tell your Auntie Helen all about it.
Barbara It's nothing.
Helen Make yourself scarce, Bob—let me talk to her alone.
Bob It's Julie and her exams.
Barbara (*gratefully following Bob's lead*) Yes, it's Julie and her exams.
Helen Don't worry about Julie—she'll be okay.
Bob They're very important, these exams.
Helen She'll be okay. You know she will. She'll do fine.
Barbara Well, I hope so.

Helen You must stop worrying, honey—otherwise you'll make yourself really ill.

Barbara Yes.

Helen I mean it.

Barbara Yes.

Helen So stop worrying, okay?

Barbara (*managing a smile*) I'll try.

Helen (*squeezing Barbara's arm*) That's my girl! (*She rises to her feet*)

Helen Where is Julie? Out with the boys?

Bob She's gone to a hockey match.

Helen If I were you, honey, I'd go upstairs and have a proper rest.

Barbara Yes, all right.

Helen Go to bed and pamper yourself. Bob'll bring you a cup of tea, won't you, Bob?

Bob Of course.

Helen Make a fuss of yourself. You deserve it. (*She pauses by the door*) Hey, listen—before I go—there's something I ought to tell you.

Barbara What's that?

Helen Peter and I have been—well, we've been thinking about the future.

Bob What about it?

Helen I've been feeling kinda low just recently—the January blues, I guess. Anyway, we both think it's time to move on.

Barbara } (*together*) { Move on ...?
Bob   }   { Move where?

Helen Peter's got some friends in Australia. We're thinking of packing our bags and going over there for six months or so. It's only an idea, of course, but Peter seems pretty keen.

Barbara and Bob exchange a brief glance

Bob Well, that's ... that's quite a big idea.

Helen Sure is. (*She grins*) Just think of it: all the sun—Bondi Beach—all those sexy young Aussies just waiting for Helen Kroger to put in an appearance. Sounds good, eh? Just poifeck.

Bob Yes, it sounds marvellous.

Barbara (*rising to her feet*) Yes, it does—it sounds marvellous.

Helen You think so?

Barbara Yes I do.

Helen (*smiling*) Trying to get rid of us, huh?

Barbara No, seriously—I think you should—it'd do you good, a change of scene ...

Helen Well, maybe.

Barbara (*urgently*) No, really—I mean it—don't ...

Helen stares at Barbara. The telephone rings. Barbara goes to the hall. Bob rightly suspects that Helen is puzzled by Barbara's uncharacteristically emotional behaviour; he tries to ease the atmosphere with a light-hearted explanation

Bob The phone never stops these days—and it's always for Julie.

Barbara (*on the telephone*) Hello? . . . Oh, hello, Maureen . . .

Bob (*grinning at Helen*) See what I mean?

Barbara (*on the telephone*) What? . . . No, she's not; she's gone down to the Sports Centre. . . . When? This evening? . . . Yes, all right. . . . Yes, I'll tell her—hang on a minute. . . . (*Writing a note*) Fourteen Hillcroft Road. . . . Yes, I'll tell her. . . . Bye-bye, Maureen, bye-bye.

Barbara replaces the receiver and returns to the sitting-room. She and Helen stand facing each other. Helen's expression is grave and concerned

Helen Are you sure there's nothing wrong?

Barbara nods

Barbara Quite sure.

Helen Well, you just let me know if there's anything I can do, okay?

Barbara nods

Take good care of her, Bob—she's a very special lady. Give my love to Julie. *Ciao.*

Helen goes out

The Lights fade

Stewart joins Barbara and Bob in the sitting-room

There is the distant sound of church bells. The Lights come up. Day

Stewart Is Julie not here?

Bob No, she's gone down to the shops. They forgot to send us the Sunday paper.

Stewart Ah. (*Brief pause*) She doesn't know . . .? She didn't see anything?

Bob No.

Stewart No—Well, there wasn't much to see, really.

A moment of awkward, uneasy silence

Bob Everything went off all right, then?

Stewart Oh yes. Absolutely according to plan. Couldn't have been better.

Bob What, um . . . (*he hesitates as if unwilling to learn the truth*) . . . what actually happened?

Stewart We picked up Lonsdale and his two chums outside the Old Vic, then we came here. It was about half-past six—perhaps you saw the car?

Bob We weren't looking.

Stewart No, well . . . Superintendent Smith told the Krogers that they were going to be arrested on suspicion of offences against the Official Secrets Act. Mrs Kroger asked if she could go and stoke the boiler before they left the house, but Mr Smith was naturally suspicious. He had a look in her handbag. He found a six-page letter in Russian, apparently from Lonsdale to his wife—a glass slide containing three microdots—and a typed sheet of numbers, presumably some sort of a code. (*A small smile*) I'm not surprised she wanted to stoke the boiler.

Barbara and Bob make no response. Brief pause

And I was right about the radio transmitter. It was hidden under the kitchen floor.

Bob Where are they now?

Stewart Bow Street Police Station.

Barbara and Bob remain silent. Stewart strolls across to the window

I'm afraid you'll have the Press poking around for a week or so—it's a damn good story, you can't blame them. But after that, all being well, you'll be left in peace.

Bob Will we have to go to court?

Stewart Oh no, there'll be no need for that. We'll see that your names aren't even mentioned.

The front door opens and Julie enters; she is carrying a Sunday newspaper

Julie Mum, what's going on?

Bob In here, Julie.

Julie enters the sitting-room

Julie Oh, hello, Mr Stewart.

Stewart Hello, Miss Jackson.

Julie (*to Barbara*) There's a whole crowd of people in Auntie Helen's house—what's going on?

Barbara Oh, Julie . . .

Stewart Yes, perhaps I should explain——

Julie (*turning to Stewart, suddenly alarmed*) Has something happened?

Stewart Yes, I'm afraid so—in fact—well, the truth is, they've been arrested.

Julie *Arrested . . .?!*

Barbara We couldn't tell you, Julie——

Bob (*overlapping*) It was for your own good.

Barbara (*overlapping*) —we couldn't tell you it was them.

Julie But why—what's happened?

Stewart They're the ones we've been watching.

Julie stares at Stewart

Julie Auntie Helen and Uncle Peter . . .?

Stewart We had to find out, you see. We had to be sure—that's why we came here.

Julie Find out *what*?

Stewart Evidence. We had to have proof that they were passing on secrets.

Julie (*aghast*) What do you mean?

Stewart They're spies. They're working for the Russians.

Silence

Julie (*barely audible*) I don't believe it.

Barbara It's true, darling . . . really, it is.

Julie gasps; her hands fly to her face; Barbara goes to her

Oh, Julie, my Julie, I'm so sorry.
Julie (*louder*) I don't believe it.
Bob Mum's right. It's true.

Barbara embraces Julie; they are both weeping

Barbara We wanted to tell you, but we couldn't. We didn't know what to do.
Julie How could she do it? How could she do it? How could she do it?
Barbara Oh, Julie, don't—please don't—please!
Julie (*her voice rising*) How could she do it how could she do it how could she do it how could she do it how could she do it how could she do it how could she . . .

Julie breaks away from Barbara and runs upstairs

Barbara (*with a terrible cry of anguish*) Julie!

The Lights fade

Bob steps forward to address the audience

Bob Julie went up to her room. She collected together all the things that Helen and Peter had ever given her—the handkerchiefs, the necklace, the silk blouse, she took them out into the garden and burnt them. (*Pause*) A few days later, Mr Stewart called round with a present for Barbara: a thank-you present, he said, for looking after his girls for all those weeks. It was a box of six fish knives and forks. Silver-plated. (*Pause*) The Krogers were sentenced to twenty years' imprisonment. Later, we discovered that Helen was a colonel in the KGB. (*Pause*) Julie's bitterness did not last. Curious to see her Auntie Helen again, she went to visit her in Holloway Prison. Towards the end of the conversation, Helen said, "I'll never forgive your mother—never." After eight years, they were released from prison in exchange for an Englishman who had been jailed by the Russians. They flew to Poland to start a new life. A crowd of journalists watched them go. "Let's all be friends," said Helen. (*Pause*) A few weeks after that, a Sunday afternoon it was, Barbara went into the kitchen, sat down on a chair, and died. A heart attack. She was so young, still in her fifties. I miss her more as time goes by. More—not less. Is it always like that?

CURTAIN

FURNITURE AND PROPERTY LIST

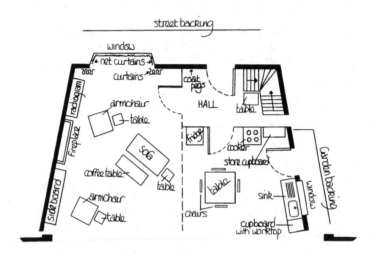

ACT I

On stage: IN HALL

Table. *On it:* telephone, pad, pen

Coat pegs by front door

IN SITTING-ROOM

Sofa. *On it:* cushions

2 armchairs

Occasional tables. *On them:* ashtrays

Coffee-table

Radiogram

Sideboard. *In it:* bottle of scotch, glasses

Window curtains (open)

Net curtains in window

Framed floral oil-paintings on wall

Fireplace. *In hearth:* electric fire. *On mantelpiece:* clock

IN KITCHEN

Table. *On it:* teapot, tea-strainer, 2 cups and saucers, 2 plates, jug of milk cutlery, newspaper for **Bob**

4 chairs

Store cupboard. *In it:* tins of food, tea caddy containing tea, jar of coffee etc.

Cupboard with worktop. *In cupboard:* cups, saucers, plates, jug. *On top:* electric kettle (practical)
Cooker
Sink unit (practical). *In drawer:* knives, spoons
Fridge. *In it:* bottle of milk. *On top:* radio, bowl of apples

Off stage: Artist's easel wrapped in tablecloth (**Helen** and **Peter**)

Personal: **Bob:** wristwatch
Barbara: wristwatch
Helen: wristwatch
Peter: wristwatch

During lighting change on page 5

Strike: Tablecloth from sitting-room
Cups, saucers, plates, cutlery, newspaper from kitchen table

Re-set: Teapot, tea-strainer on worktop
Jug of milk in fridge

Off stage: Dress **(Barbara)**
Dress **(Helen)**
School satchel **(Julie)**

During lighting change on page 13

Strike: Unfinished dress, **Julie**'s gloves and scarf from kitchen

Re-set: Window curtains closed

Personal: **Stewart:** wristwatch, photograph, notepad, pen, packet of cigarettes, lighter

During lighting change on page 20

Set: Newspaper for **Bob**, sewing for **Barbara**

During lighting change on page 23

Strike: Newspaper, sewing

Re-set: Window curtains open

During Black-out on page 32

Strike: Used glass from sitting-room

Re-set: Window curtains open

Set: Oil-paints, brushes, palette, canvas on easel

Off stage: Vegetables **(Barbara)**
Shopping basket **(Helen)**

ACT II

Strike: Vegetables from kitchen table

Off stage: Shopping bags containing tinned food, sausages, groceries etc. **(Barbara)**
Cake-tin **(Helen)**

Personal: **Sally:** umbrella

During Black-out on page 40

Strike: All items from kitchen table
Oil-paints, brushes, palette from easel

Re-set: Window curtains closed

Off stage: Shopping bag containing oil-paints, brushes, palette **(Barbara)**

During lighting change on page 48

Strike: Shopping bag, used glasses from sitting-room

Re-set: Oil-paints, brushes, palette by easel, window curtains open

Set: Cardboard box, tissue paper, now-completed dress in sitting-room

During lighting change on page 52

Strike: Cardboard box, tissue paper, folded dress from sitting-room

Re-set: Window curtains closed

Set: Decorated Christmas tree in sitting-room
Bottle of sherry, glasses on coffee-table

During lighting change on page 55

Strike: Decorated Christmas tree, used glasses, bottle of sherry from sitting-room

Re-set: Window curtains open

Off stage: Unplugged telephone **(Sally)**
Sunday newspaper **(Julie)**

LIGHTING PLOT

Practical fittings required: electric fire, pendant light, coloured lights on Christmas tree

A sitting-room, kitchen and hall. The same scene throughout

ACT I

To open: Spot downstage on **Bob**

Cue 1	**Bob:** "It was marvellous." *Cross fade to overall morning light*	(Page 1)
Cue 2	**Barbara:** "Oh, Helen, dear Helen—you're priceless!" *Cross fade to spot downstage on* **Stewart**	(Page 5)
Cue 3	**Stewart:** "It is, by the way, by and large—true." *Fade spot. When ready bring up overall dusk lighting*	(Page 5)
Cue 4	**Barbara** switches on the electric fire *Bring up red glow effect from electric fire*	(Page 6)
Cue 5	**Bob:** "Right." *Cross fade to spot downstage on* **Peter**	(Page 13)
Cue 6	**Peter:** "—Julie especially." *Cross fade to general interior lighting in hall and sitting-room areas with pendant light and electric fire glow*	(Page 13)
Cue 7	**Stewart:** "I think you'll like her." *Cross fade to spot downstage on* **Thelma**	(Page 20)
Cue 8	**Thelma** exits *Cross fade to general interior lighting in hall and sitting-room areas with pendant light and electric fire glow*	(Page 21)
Cue 9	**Bob:** "She'll have gone." *Cross fade to spot downstage on* **Barbara**	(Page 23)
Cue 10	**Barbara:** "... I could feel his hands trembling." *Cross fade to overall general afternoon light, gradually fading as scene progresses*	(Page 23)
Cue 11	**Barbara** draws the curtains *Dim lighting*	(Page 31)
Cue 12	**Barbara** switches on the light *Snap on pendant and covering light in sitting-room*	(Page 31)
Cue 13	**Barbara** walks past **Bob** and goes to the kitchen *Fade to Black-out. When ready bring up overall daylight effect*	(Page 32)

ACT II

To open: Overall daylight effect

Cue 14   **Barbara:** "—just leave me alone!"   (Page 40)
            *Fade to Black-out. When ready bring up general interior lighting
                in hall, kitchen and sitting-room with pendant light and electric
                fire glow*

Cue 15   **Barbara:** ". . . I'll bring it in."   (Page 48)
            Cross fade to spot downstage on **Barbara**

Cue 16   **Barbara:** "And she was right—they didn't."   (Page 48)
            Cross fade to overall general late afternoon light

Cue 17   **Barbara** sobs   (Page 52)
            Cross fade to spot downstage on **Peter**

Cue 18   **Peter:** "That evening, my whole life changed."   (Page 53)
            *Cross fade to general interior lighting in hall and sitting-room
                areas with all practicals on*

Cue 19   Eventually **Barbara** joins in the singing   (Page 55)
            Cross fade to spot downstage on **Helen**

Cue 20   **Helen:** ". . . there was no turning back."   (Page 55)
            *Fade to Black-out. When ready bring up overall general daylight
                effect*

Cue 21   **Helen** goes out   (Page 61)
            *Fade to Black-out. When ready bring up overall general daylight
                effect*

Cue 22   **Barbara:** "Julie!"   (Page 63)
            Cross fade to spot downstage on **Bob**

EFFECTS PLOT

Please read the notice on page viii concerning the use of copyright material.

ACT I

Cue 1	**Barbara:** "You like cornflakes." *Doorbell*	(Page 3)
Cue 2	**Barbara:** "—someone of your age ..." *Telephone*	(Page 9)
Cue 3	**Barbara:** "—and supposing——" *Doorbell*	(Page 14)
Cue 4	**Stewart:** "... in this part of the world." *Telephone*	(Page 16)
Cue 5	**Bob** resumes reading his newspaper; **Barbara** sews *Clock strikes half-hour*	(Page 22)
Cue 6	**Barbara:** "You know it is." *Telephone*	(Page 32)
Cue 7	As the Lights come up *Music from the radio*	(Page 32)
Cue 8	**Barbara** enters from the garden *Doorbell*	(Page 33)
Cue 9	**Barbara** switches off the radio *Cut radio music; doorbell rings*	(Page 33)
Cue 10	**Barbara** stands motionless by the window *Doorbell*	(Page 33)

ACT II

Cue 11	**Thelma:** "That voice." *Doorbell*	(Page 38)
Cue 12	**Julie** exits upstairs *Door slam*	(Page 52)
Cue 13	**Helen** kisses **Julie** on the forehead *Telephone*	(Page 54)
Cue 14	**Stewart** and **Bob** follow **Barbara** to the sitting-room *Doorbell*	(Page 58)
Cue 15	**Barbara:** "Well, it is." *Doorbell*	(Page 58)

Cue 16 **Helen** stares at **Barbara**   (Page 60)
       Telephone

Cue 17 The Lights fade   (Page 61)
       Distant sound of church bells. Continue for part of scene

MADE AND PRINTED IN GREAT BRITAIN BY
LATIMER TREND & COMPANY LTD PLYMOUTH

MADE IN ENGLAND